Praise for *Slow*

"*Slow* is a breakthrough  es that anyone can benefit from ...s have taught. Lee makes it acc... Chopra
author

"*Slow* explores the core causes of modern malaise and provides clear and actionable steps on how to fix it. I learned so much from this book. A wake-up call on how to slow down and smell the Qi."

James Nestor
bestselling author of *Breath*

"Lee Holden is a remarkable teacher. I consistently recommend his work to family and friends. My father, for example, had his backspin disappear by doing Lee's slow movement practices. Highly recommended."

Vishen Lakhiani
New York Times bestselling author and CEO of Mindvalley

"Lee is truly an inspiration. He always amazes me in how he takes ancient wisdom and makes it accessible. *Slow* is genius."

Mantak Chia
founder of Universal Healing Tao and bestselling author

"Lee Holden is a gifted teacher of body wisdom and our ability to harness our energy to live with more vitality. In his new book, he offers us the power of slow and shares numerous transformational practices to follow the ancient rhythm of wellness. Embrace slow and embrace a wiser, healthier way of being."

Doug Abrams
New York Times bestselling coauthor of *The Book of Joy*

"Lee is a gift. I use his program to start every day. In less than fifteen minutes, I feel amazing and am ready to start my day. I have more energy at 82 years old than I did at 35."

Eleanor Coppola
Emmy-winning director, author, and artist

"Lee is a true master of internal energy practices. *Slow* creates a harmonious inner environment through the body, mind, and spirit. Highly recommended."

Marie Diamond
feng shui master and author featured in *The Secret*

"Lee is a natural on TV. His poise and lighthearted nature have made him a regular fixture on American Public Television. I've enjoyed working with him for the last ten years."

Eric Robertson
former CEO of American Public Television

"Lee's program on health and healing is in the Top 5 list of all-time customer satisfaction for Sounds True. He is a joy to work with."

Tami Simon
founder of Sounds True

"Lee gives us simple ways to use Eastern wisdom for modern life. *Slow* is a wonderful 'hack' to living your best life."

Dave Asprey
founder of Bulletproof and four-time *New York Times* bestselling author

"*Slow* is the perfect antidote to the chaos of our overscheduled and constantly rushed modern lives. Holden's insightful book—rooted in his lifelong career as Qi Gong and meditation master—offers a refreshing approach to reclaiming tranquility and presence, providing practical methods to slow down and savor each moment. If you are ready to break free from the frantic pace and rediscover the joy of living fully and intentionally, this is a must-read."

Juliet Starrett
New York Times bestselling coauthor of *Built to Move*

"In the hallowed pages of *Slow*, Lee Holden not only lives up to his revered reputation but transcends it, offering us a portal into the profound wisdom that has defined his journey as a Qi Gong master. What a divine gift it is to delve into this book, where each word beckons us to slow down, breathe deeply, and realign with the sacred rhythm of life—a rhythm that Lee has so masterfully captured and now generously shares with us all."

Maureen J. St. Germain
award-winning author and founder of St. Germain Mystery School

slow

Also by Lee Holden

7 Minutes of Magic: The Ultimate Energy Workout

Taoist Sexual Energy: Harness Your Qi Energy for Ecstasy, Vitality, and Transformation (with Rachel Carlton Abrams)

slow

How to Improve Your Energy, Health and Relationships Through the Power of Slow

LEE HOLDEN

American Qi Gong Master and Author of
7 Minutes of Magic

RIDER

RIDER

UK | USA | Canada | Ireland | Australia
India | New Zealand | South Africa

Rider is part of the Penguin Random House group of companies
whose addresses can be found at global.penguinrandomhouse.com

Penguin Random House UK
One Embassy Gardens, 8 Viaduct Gardens, London SW11 7BW

penguin.co.uk
global.penguinrandomhouse.com

First published in Great Britain by Rider in 2025
First published in the United States of America by Sounds True in 2025

1

Copyright © Lee Holden 2025

The moral right of the author has been asserted.

No part of this book may be used or reproduced in any manner for the purpose
of training artificial intelligence technologies or systems. In accordance with
Article 4(3) of the DSM Directive 2019/790, Penguin Random House expressly
reserves this work from the text and data mining exception.

The information in this book has been compiled as general guidance on the specific
subjects addressed. It is not a substitute and not to be relied on for medical or healthcare
professional advice. So far as the author is aware the information given is correct and
up to date as at November 2024. Practice, laws and regulations all change and the reader
should obtain up-to-date professional advice on any such issues. The author and
publishers disclaim, as far as the law allows, any liability arising directly or indirectly
from the use or misuse of the information contained in this book.

Typeset by Jouve (UK), Milton Keynes
Printed and bound in Great Britain by Clays Ltd, Elcograf S.p.A.

The authorised representative in the EEA is Penguin Random House Ireland,
Morrison Chambers, 32 Nassau Street, Dublin D02 YH68

A CIP catalogue record for this book is available from the British Library

ISBN 9781846048470

Penguin Random House is committed to a sustainable future
for our business, our readers and our planet. This book is made
from Forest Stewardship Council® certified paper.

Contents

Introduction   1

The Slow Method   3

Welcome to the Slow Revolution!   7

The Myth That Faster Is Better   11

From Autopilot to Mindful Mastery   15

Choosing Bliss over Busy   19

PRINCIPLE 1: SLOW MIND   23

Stress: Your Modern-Day Inheritance   25

Are You Stressed?   27

The Bear and the Big Silver Lining of Stress   31
    EXERCISE #1: First Aid for Stress: Primal Shaking   33

Mindfulness: The Number-One Enemy of Stress   35

Welcome to the Mindful Tea Shop   39
    EXERCISE #2: The Mindful Tea Ritual   40

Autopilot and the Drunken Teenage Monkey   43

If You Can Worry, You Can Meditate   47

A Thank-You Note   49
    EXERCISE #3: Gratitude Meditation   52

Mindfulness Meditation: Where Are You?   55
    EXERCISE #4: The "Where Am I?" Meditation   57

Why Do You Want to Live Here, Anyway?   59
    EXERCISE #5: Make Your Mindfulness List   61

Your Mind Is a Garden   63

PRINCIPLE 2: SLOW BODY   65

The Surprising Physical Impact of a Slow Practice   69

Relax: Your Plane Will Take Off Without Your Help   71

Let Go of Control, and Go with the Flow   73

Surfing into Flow   75

Channeling Your Inner Bruce Lee   77
    EXERCISE #6: The "Go Slow, Enter the Flow" Qi Gong Sequence   78

If You Are Forced to Sit on Your Butt All Day   81
    EXERCISE #7: Qi Break: Spinal-Cord Breathing   82

Why It's Time for You to Go "Au Naturel"   83
    EXERCISE #8: Slow Down with Nature's Big Five   85

Going Deeper: Fuel for the Body   91

Why Do We Stuff Our Bodies at the Buffet?   93

Barbara's Revolution   95

Eat S-L-O-W-L-Y   97
    EXERCISE #9: The 32-Second Chew Rule   100

Pleasure Through Food   101
    EXERCISE #10: Mealtime Mindfulness   102

Combating Fast-Eating Habits with Acupressure   105
    EXERCISE #11: Ear Acupressure to Cut Cravings   106
    EXERCISE #12: Acupressure for Optimal Digestion   107

A Note on Binge Eating   109

Additional Tips for Those Drawn to Binge Eating   111

Slow Eating Is the New Black   113

The Breath as Medicine: Taking Your Vitamin O   115

How Should You Be Breathing Right Now?   119
    EXERCISE #13: The 5.5 Breathing Rule   120

Breathing and Your Emotional Landscape   123
    EXERCISE #14: Vagal Breathing: The Breath of Joy   124

Breaking the Ice with Wim Hof   127
    EXERCISE #15: Go Fast to Go Slow Breathing   129

Why You Need to Shut Your Mouth   131
    EXERCISE #16: Getting Friendly with Your Nasal Passages   133

Breathe, Just Breathe 135

To the Heart of the Matter 137

PRINCIPLE 3: SLOW RELATIONSHIPS 139

Connection: The Self and Others 143

Slow Self-Love 145

Self-Love Defined 151
 EXERCISE #17: Heartfulness 152
 EXERCISE #18: Mirror Work 153

Cultivating Slow, Deep Connections with Others 157
 EXERCISE #19: Slow Down Conflict 158
 EXERCISE #20: Mindful Relating 163

Slow Communication 165

A Note on Conflict 169
 EXERCISE #21: Conscious Communication Boot Camp 170

Slow Intimacy 173

Taoist Sexual Secrets 177

Slow Sexual Courtship 181
 EXERCISE #22: Energy Exchange 183
 EXERCISE #23: Sexual Reflexology 183
 EXERCISE #24: Microcosmic Orbit Breathing 188
 EXERCISE #25: Fusing Jing Qi with a Partner 189

What's Love Got to Do with It? 193

PRINCIPLES UNITE: YOUR SLOW DAILY ROUTINE 195

Your Slow Daily Routine 197

Creating Your Daily Slow Routine 207

The Slow Life: Closing Words 209

ACKNOWLEDGMENTS 213

NOTES 215

ABOUT THE AUTHOR 225

Introduction

> The soft overcomes the hard.
> The slow overcomes the fast.
> Let your workings remain a mystery.
> Just show people the results.
>
> —Lao Tzu, Tao Te Ching, Verse 36

Imagine for a second that you hurried through the most precious moments of your life. Having your fortieth birthday dinner at your favorite restaurant would be a battle against the clock. There you'd be, eating as swiftly as possible, scarfing down that freshly caught lobster and caviar like a golden retriever who hasn't been fed in days. Imagine chugging that premium Italian glass of wine, whose grapes were slowly grown in the mountains of Sicily . . . like a dry-mouthed runner at the end of a half-marathon.

And then there's that romantic night in the bedroom with your partner. You burst open the door, not because of your uncontrollable passion. Oh, no. You've got no time for sexy entrances. No time for sweet nothings and gentle caresses. No time for romance. Instead, you both engage in a clumsy, rapid fumble through intimacy, skipping the buildup and crossing the finish line as quickly as possible before briskly falling asleep.

How about that trip to Paris you've always dreamed of? You get to the airport and hop in a cab, which zooms all over the city at record speed, just enough to catch a glimpse of the Eiffel Tower, the exterior of the Louvre, and the underbelly of the Arc de Triomphe, before speedily delivering you back to the airport.

Paris? Tick.

Sounds ridiculous, right? But let's not hoodwink ourselves into thinking that we don't do a less dramatic variation of this with the gift that is our daily life.

Nobody wants to rush around like a headless chicken, yet this is how modern life tends to feel. What we actually *want* to do is to slow down, savor the beautiful moments of life, create more of them, and make them last as long as possible. We all want to relax more, stress less, and live in a state of inner peace. We all want to create more special moments in time where the beauty of the moment unfolds, blossoms into presence, connection, and bliss. We want to drink the sweet nectar of life and live it to the max, in full health, with vibrant energy, enthusiasm, love, joy, and happiness. And that requires a different pace, which requires *slowing down*.

That's not to say that after reading this book, you won't lead a very productive life or be able to act quickly when you need to. Slowing down doesn't equate with laziness and sloth; rather it fuels our endeavors in a way that stress never could. I've seen it happen a thousand times, and a thousand times again, in the clients I've worked with over thirty years of Slow Method practice.

The Slow Method

The Slow Method has three unique elements taken from the wisdom of many forms of Eastern meditation, Chinese martial arts, and Taoist philosophies. All of these timeless practices are incredible tools to optimize modern life. These ideas are far from new, but this book is the first of its kind to bring all the slowness principles together in a way that's accessible and practical for everyone.

So what is the Slow Method? It's a collection of revolutionary yet simple practices that can be broken down into three simple principles:

- Principle 1: Slow Mind
- Principle 2: Slow Body
- Principle 3: Slow Relationships

These practices have changed my life and the lives of countless others. We now have a million-strong community forming part of the Slow Revolution, and it's growing every day. I've dedicated thirty years of my life to teaching well-being through slowness, and I've seen the results firsthand. Miracles happen when we ease off the throttle.

The Slow Method was born at Golden Gate Park in San Francisco. The sun was rising and shining through the misty marine layer, and the slow-moving fog brought about a feeling of stillness and awe within me. I was nineteen at the time, and I happened to be sitting on a bench watching a group of the most peaceful people I'd ever seen.

They moved and flowed in unison, with peace and grace. They looked as if they were part of nature itself, moving with as much lightness as the wind through the trees. I remember asking myself, *What on Earth are they doing?*

This question set me off on a journey of discovery that transformed my mind, body, and soul and set the foundation for the Slow Method you'll learn in this book. The practices of Qi Gong and Tai Chi (which you'll see people doing in every park in China as well as San Francisco) taught me countless valuable lessons, but among the most important was that my mind and body were intrinsically connected. If I slowed my body, my mind would follow. And if I slowed my racing mind, my body could, and would, respond. It was from that place of inner balance and self-care, I would later learn, that out-of-this-world relationships with others could bloom.

Qi Gong has been called "the art of effortless power" and originated some five thousand years ago in ancient China. Qi signifies life-force energy, referring to a mysterious force, an electricity, that courses through the mind and the body, creating movement and animation. Qi is the electrical impulse that beats the heart. Qi is the light in the mind that creates images. Qi is the power that moves through the organs, muscles, ligaments, and bones.

The Qi Gong masters used their bodies to mirror the movements of nature—the way a cloud would float across the sky or the river would flow down the mountain or the tree would sway in the wind. This allowed practitioners to feel connected to all of life: life all around them and the life within them.

Qi Gong was the precursor to practices like Tai Chi, which uses the same principles—relaxation, slowness, flow, and energy—as its foundation. The application and history of Tai Chi are related more to martial arts, whereas Qi Gong is more of an energy cultivation practice for health and healing. Both Qi Gong and Tai Chi move the body slowly, rhythmically, and with the full self (integration of body, mind, emotion, and energy) to create the feeling of wholeness.

The body and mind are two instruments in the symphony of the self, and practices like Qi Gong, mindfulness, and meditation are like the expert conductors, creating harmony among the individual instruments. This interested me more than anything else ever had. I went on to train with many different master teachers of Qi Gong and Taoist philosophy (more on that later), including Master Mantak Chia. At the age of twenty-four, after graduating in psychology from the University of California, Berkeley, I found myself at his healing arts center in Thailand. Mantak Chia is one of the world's foremost authorities in Eastern esoteric practices. And it was under his loving wing that, in his own words, I went from a student to a master myself. Now it's your turn.

Welcome to the Slow Revolution!

The Qi Gong masters of antiquity all agreed that when you slow down, you absorb more positive, life-giving energy, something we're in dire need of. This is called "acquiring Qi." We all absorb energy without even being conscious of it in modern life, although we tend to acquire the not-so-pleasurable type of Qi instead, picking up stress, anxiety, other people's negative vibes, and low-frequency emotional energy. We go quickly, get caught up in whirlwinds of negativity, and move fast *in the wrong direction*. We work hard but rarely get what we truly want. We are striving for more productivity and wealth but end up with a lack of purpose. Consequently, we feel exhausted, with no skills to soak up the good stuff again.

In this book, I delve into what I call "Quick Myths," misguided beliefs that often result in this depleted or negative Qi, burnout, and disconnection. You'll encounter several sections dedicated to exposing these myths, each one followed by a "Slow Reality" segment. These sections serve as mental Post-it notes aimed at embedding lasting insights in your long-term memory.

Through the three principles you're about to learn, you'll start acquiring more of the Qi you actually want: peace, love, vitality, health, healing, tranquility, connection, and general positivity (called "righteous Qi"). You'll begin to absorb it on a regular basis in everything you do—so much so that these states of being will become part of who you are.

The best part? It will happen effortlessly. There's no need for extreme changes in your life. The tools you're about to learn go far beyond a series of Qi Gong movements, as you'll find in my previous book, *7 Minutes of Magic*. Although some basic exercises are included in *Slow*, many of the exercises I'll ask you to do include changing the *how* of your daily activities, as opposed to the *what*. The Slow Method works with the life you already have, making small, incremental changes to the way you live and relate. By the time you finish this book, you'll feel it in your body. You'll feel it in your breath. You'll feel it in your mind. And you will feel it in your relationships, including the one you have with yourself.

Living slow rebels against the status quo and is the key to achieving *anything* our hearts truly desire.

QUICK MYTH: In order to get more positive energy, you need to immediately make a huge effort to transform everything: quit your job, get a different partner, palm off your kids as much as you can, and set completely different goals. Be a new person!

SLOW REALITY: Real change comes when we make small yet purposeful changes to the *way* we live our lives. It's all about living with slowness, with flow, and with mindfulness, bringing value to yourself as you are and shining a light on the magic that is already present in your life.

Throughout this book, I will share the principles, and proven methodologies, for accessing the magical benefits of slowing down. I'll do so in clear, practical ways that will help you create lasting change in your mind, body, and relationships, that is, your life as well as the lives of your loved ones. We will address topics ranging from rewiring the mind to combating stress and anxiety to connecting deeply with those you love—your friends, family, colleagues, and romantic partner if you have one. The mind chapter has a special focus on your psychology and emotional landscape, the body chapter on your physical well-being and energy levels, and the relationship chapter on self-love, conscious communication, and sex. Most of the sexual content and tools included in this book can be used with or without a partner, so don't feel put off if you're single.

My hope is that after reading this book, you'll have all the tools you'll ever need to redesign your mind, body, and relationships for the better, and in a way that brings forth the best aspects of yourself.

This book centers on nurturing and reshaping the most exceptional aspects of the human experience. It guides you to embrace more of those heightened experiences of love and joy, extend their duration, and skillfully create moments that will be etched in your memory forever.

At the end of the day, your life is just that: *yours*. And it's time we start living our lives with mastery, as opposed to remaining bound to the clock.

Modern life can be wild, can't it? We often have the pedal to the metal, giving it all the gas we possibly can with the other foot pressing firmly on the brake. We are using up our fuel and getting nowhere. *Nowhere*. But our capitalist society tells us to keep going, to speed up and go ever faster on an intangible treadmill that doesn't seem to have a STOP button. Why?

The Myth That Faster Is Better

The pervasive myth that faster is somehow better wreaks havoc on our mind, body, and most precious relationships.

Do it faster, do more of it, and finish the job in record time. Daily life strives for speed.

Technology sells the illusion that if we buy a "better" smartphone that carries out the most complex tasks as well as having four different cameras and a robot that can do a backflip and beat a chess master at her own game in record time, we will be stress-free, entertained, and happy. If we develop AI to manage the mundane, self-functioning factories that shoot out plastic products more optimally than human hands ever could and talking speakers that have a name and know what we need to buy online before we do, life will be a breeze.

In actuality, we have all of this right now. Yet despite these major advances in technology, we still scurry from one moment to another at a frantic, hectic pace, trying our best to get through our day and cross items off our dreaded, never-ending to-do lists. Just look around you. Is it just me, or does it seem that society is getting more stressed out, burned out, unhappy, sick, overweight, and depressed? Unfortunately, the statistics back me up. I'll share them with you later.

That said, as opposed to merely surviving our daily experience and getting it over and done with as quickly as possible, I do believe there exists a vastly improved approach. Drawing on the philosophical wisdom of the East and merging it with Western science, I advocate the notion that rather than just surviving, humanity is capable of thriving.

This doesn't mean changing *what* we're doing per se but rather the way we go about doing it. By slowing down and bringing rhythm and harmony into our daily experience without compromising our productivity, our levels of well-being would skyrocket. And the dismissive idea that "we have bigger fish to fry" than tending to our 360° health is a total misunderstanding of the importance of well-being.

Let's step back and look at the goal of life. What is it exactly that we are all striving to achieve? Although our dreams wear many masks, what most people want for themselves and their loved ones, more than anything else, is to be healthy and happy.

Is modern life helping us achieve those things? For the majority, the answer is no. Not by a long shot.

In defense of modern life, it's undeniable that it has helped us grow and develop. The American dream has inspired contentment in many, at least in the short term, and has encouraged us to achieve a steady income, build a solid career, and have a fruitful family life. There's nothing wrong with that. What's more, technology has supported those of us who work remotely, and the same devices that give us the means to work have gifted us with instant audio and video communication with our nearest and dearest no matter where they are in the world. Then there's medicine. I'm a huge advocate of Chinese medicine and acupuncture, but the moment you break your arm, are injured in a car crash, or have a severe infection, you shouldn't rely on herbs. You'd be going to the hospital, an establishment that wouldn't exist without cutting-edge modern research. And within hours, you'd be on the mend. Modern life can be miraculous, and the list of its benefits is long.

Long, not infinite. Despite rapid advances in medicine, for example, we have more illnesses to deal with than ever before. Cancer is on the rise. Furthermore, approximately 42 percent of recently detected cancer cases in the United States, amounting to approximately 805,600 cases in the year 2022, may have been totally preventable with lifestyle changes. This includes around 19 percent of cancer cases attributed to smoking and at least 18 percent of cases resulting from a combination of factors such as alcohol consumption, an unhealthy diet, and a lack of exercise and physical activity.[1]

The rate of depression (now considered to be a disability), especially in the younger generation, is also increasing astronomically each year. Currently, depression is said to be one of the leading causes of many other disabilities worldwide, and according to the World Health Organization, around 280 million people around the globe are currently suffering from this mental health condition. That number of people is equivalent to approximately 83 percent of the entire population of the United States.[2]

It's safe to say that despite our incredible innovations, people experience more stress and illness, have less energy, and are too busy to spend time with those they love. Furthermore, many people are fixated on their personal devices and are becoming more and more disconnected from nature, each other, and their purpose in life. More on that later. In a nutshell, we're depleted and stressed out. We are wired but inexplicably tired. Modern life with all its cutting-edge technology, despite all its promises, hasn't helped create the thriving human race it promised.

> **QUICK MYTH:** Living life in the fast lane and being busy gets you where you want to go in life. When it comes to living life to the max, it's all about hustle!
>
> **SLOW REALITY:** Slowing down helps you enjoy life as it is right now and have a clear, informed vision of where you want to go in the future.

From Autopilot to Mindful Mastery

Martin lay in the hospital bed, flipping stations on the TV remote. It was all he had energy for.

He had just had a bone-marrow transplant after being diagnosed with a rare form of leukemia. The doctors had just told him to get his affairs in order because he had about six months left to live. Martin was understandably depressed and defeated. He had formerly been a successful airline pilot and had never imagined that he'd end up dying before his fiftieth birthday.

Despite having traveled all over the world, Martin sadly hadn't truly experienced any of it. He had seen the beautiful planet from the air, through the curved cockpit window, but he hadn't had nearly enough time with his feet solidly planted on the earth. At each airport, there was always a frantic rush to exit the plane, speed-walk to the next gate, and fly another aircraft to a new, exotic destination that he'd never get to actually see. He often made the choice to work overtime rather than relax and enjoy some of the stunning places that he had the golden opportunity to visit. He had been to more than one hundred distinct paradises countless times but was just too much of a businessman to notice.

For years, stress, anxiety, and speed had been his default states, causing him to become a pilot constantly running *on autopilot*. He was immersed in the rat race in the sky—one he thought he could win. The ugly truth is that nobody ever does. Life isn't a game to be won but a gift and a pleasure to be lived in the moment.

Martin lay in bed desperately wishing he had made different choices. He had made lots of money and had worked hard. He had made it big in the airline travel sector, and he was highly respected by many. *But at what cost?*

His work had taken him away from his family—his wife and two beautiful daughters. He'd neglected his partner in many ways and had missed some of the most precious moments of his daughters' lives. Eventually, the stress of his constant professional responsibilities had led to a nasty and expensive divorce. Martin had chosen not to engage in the court battle his wife had threatened him with if he didn't give in to her financial demands. *After all*, he thought, *I can always earn more money*. But he hadn't had a chance to. And according to the doctors, he never would. While lying in the hospital bed, Martin stopped his busy thumb on the remote. On the TV screen appeared a man who seemed to be floating on water. He was standing in the middle of a stream on a plank, eyes closed, practicing what looked like slow martial art movements.

Martin had once seen a group of elderly people practicing the same sorts of graceful, slow, rhythmic movements in the local park, but he had never understood what exactly they were doing or why. He watched, transfixed, as the instructor gently recited poetic descriptions of the movements like "Cloudy Hands" and "Pebble in the Pond."

His shoulders dropped away from his ears as he watched.

He forgot about the pain in his body for a few minutes. His diagnosis, the hospital bed, and his loneliness slipped his mind as he melted into the moment. From his bed, he started moving his arms in the way the instructor did on the screen, slowly, with relaxation, and with a profound sense of flow. "Thanks for joining me in this Qi Gong tutorial," said the instructor after the class was over, bowing in reverence. Martin found himself bowing back, at total peace, yet curiously wondering what "Qi Gong" was supposed to mean. He searched for it on his phone. He was informed that Qi Gong was an ancient Chinese practice that combined movement, breath control, and meditation to cultivate and balance the body's vital energy, known as "Qi." The term

"Qi" refers to the life force or energy that is believed to flow through all living beings. "Gong" means "skill," so Qi Gong can be translated as "skillful cultivation of life energy." Who knew you could get more energy by slowing down?

Interesting. Well, whatever it was or wherever it came from, it worked. He felt more chilled out than ever, despite his anxiety-producing state of health. The slowness of the movements had calmed not just his body but also his *mind*. He immediately ordered the program from the public television station and slowly started to practice Qi Gong every day in the hospital.

At first, moving was difficult. He tired easily, and on particularly tough days, Martin would simply visualize the flowing movements in his head because his body was just too exhausted and overwhelmed to keep up. Over time, things eventually got easier. And little by little, he was able to move his upper body with ease. Martin loved how the slow movements made him feel, and he indulged in the enjoyment of moments of pure presence—the respites when he wasn't divorced, sick, or dying . . . the moments when he had no label hanging around his neck. The moments where he was nothing but one with the energy and flow of life.

A few weeks passed, and Martin was discharged from the hospital. Contrary to what the doctors had predicted, his health wasn't rapidly deteriorating into an inevitable demise. Neither was his health just stable. Instead, against all odds, he was getting better and better. After a few months of practice, Martin felt better than he could remember. He had more energy, he felt stronger emotionally, his mind was clear, and he even felt hope for the future. He thought it odd that this was the first time in his life that he'd ever truly felt a sense of optimism, as he'd just been given a few months to live and a stern "You need to get your affairs in order" from his doctor. It seemed that slowing down with Qi Gong had worked harmoniously with modern medicine to produce healing.

When I first met Martin at one of my Slow Method Qi Gong retreats, he was larger than life. He shook my hand with a beaming smile, telling me that I had changed his life. The Qi Gong instructor he'd seen from his hospital bed had been me, of course, although at the time, I was oblivious to his story. Nevertheless, he was emphatic that slowing down had somehow revived him and brought him back from the "brink."

A few days later, onstage in front of the entire class, Martin went on to share his full story. With tears in his eyes as he spoke earnestly into the microphone, he smiled as he told us that now, a year and a half after the original diagnosis, he was in remission. I was completely taken aback by his story and offered him a warm embrace as he stepped offstage.

Martin is now five years cancer-free and teaching the three-part Slow Method you'll find in this book. He's become a messenger of hope and a beacon of light for anyone who may have lost hope in the power of healing and the beauty of life. Thanks to the practice of living life slowly, Martin now experiences every day to the maximum, having left the state of autopilot far behind.

There is tremendous power in slowing down, and it has the capacity to change lives through deep healing and transformation, as you can see in Martin's story. But it also changes the little things, like the pleasures to be found at the dinner table with your family, intimate time with your partner, and the way you show up at the office or for your clients. Paradoxically, slowing down allows you to access peace, happiness, and well-being *faster*.

Slowing down, quite simply, is the antidote to the pressure of modern life and all the challenges that come with it.

QUICK MYTH: You have to do things in life that you don't like to be successful, and success equals financial prosperity.

SLOW REALITY: Chronically deprioritizing your well-being through an autopilot, fast-paced lifestyle in order to "be successful" can be risky to your health.

Choosing Bliss over Busy

I acknowledge that Martin's story may be triggering for some people. And if you're someone who has lost a loved one to disease, anecdotes like these can be hard to read. My intention here isn't to sell you the notion that slowing down will cure any ailment at any stage. But what I have observed with my own eyes, time and time again, is that living life slowly, in the mind, the body, and within relationships, has a catalytic effect on healing. And practicing what you're about to learn in this book will give you the keys to well-being and therefore to peace, love, and joy. That said, it is you, of course, who must use those keys to open the doors.

Many people believe that they're too busy to prioritize slowing down. But the reality is this: you *do* have time for what you're about to learn, no matter how hectic life seems. And the reason you have time is that the vast majority of the Slow Method is applicable to habits you already have. It's *how* you live that changes, not necessarily *what* you do on a daily basis. And it starts with reframing your responsibilities. In fact, a close friend of mine, John, is a shining example of someone who went from toxic-level busy to genuine bliss. Back in 2018, we got together for a cup of tea. After ordering our leaves of choice, we sat down at the table, and I asked how he was.

"Busy" was the answer. It had been for years.

This was the reply I'd expected, not only due to the fact that John had given me the same reply for just over four years but also because of his visible tension. His body language was screaming a resounding

"HELP ME! I'M STRESSED OUT, AND I DON'T KNOW IF I HAVE TIME FOR THIS TEA!" He was trying his hardest to hide this, of course, slapping on a brave face, stirring the teapot with vigor, and laughing nervously. Behind his smile, I could see the strain in his eyes and in his jaw while he desperately attempted to redirect my attention with various exuberant inquiries into *my* life: "Anyway, tell me about you, Lee. How are the kids?" He exuded anxiety like an overheated engine. After a little coaxing, John eventually opened up and shared his circumstances with me. His wife had asked for a divorce two months previously. And to rub salt in the wound, this unforeseen tragedy entailed moving out of his family home and working two jobs to cobble together the cash to keep taking care of the kids and start renting a new place.

"You really do have a lot on your plate, my friend," I said. "You need to slow down, brother."

"No way," he replied. "I'm way too busy."

It's all too common for us to succumb to the pressure, and label, of being "too busy" to look after ourselves these days. It's become the go-to answer that many of us modern humans give to an earnest *How are you?* We give it proudly, as a badge of honor, sipping our double espresso with a flustered yet triumphant grin. Busyness can signify importance and executive-level responsibility, after all. But it also implies stress, hurry, rush, anxiety, impatience, and a constant sense of a lack of time. If giving you an extra few hours in the day or an extra day in the week was the promise of this book, everyone everywhere would want a copy. But the act of simply slowing down reaps the same results, giving one a strong sense of more time and space to play with.

What's more, when you think about it, being busy implies that you're doing and taking actions that you *have* to do but don't really *want* to do. It's being led by the responsibility of the head rather than the bliss of the heart. When I look up "busy" in the dictionary, I find words like "slaving," "buried," and "assiduous." I don't know about you, but I'd prefer to pass on all that.

I asked John what he would be doing if he wasn't so busy. He laughed. I could see the sparkle come back into his eyes for just a moment. He said he'd like to travel, ride his bike, spend quality time with his kids, and just relax at the beach with a good book once in a while. Surprise, surprise—the exact opposite of being busy. They're classic examples of simple, enjoyable, and accessible ways to spend time mindfully and heartfully.

"You've got too much on your plate and too much at stake not to slow down," I told him. The comment inspired an inquisitiveness in John, making him cock his head to the side in a way that reminded me of my dog, Charlie, when he heard a strange sound. I smiled. "By slowing down, you will gain time, energy, focus, and clarity," I continued. "I know it sounds too good to be true, that somehow slowing down will lead to more productivity. But the research is out. Slowing down does that and way more."

I went on to show John a few of the slow techniques you're about to read in this book. They were game changers for him over the subsequent months. John still has a busy life to this day, but now he has strategically inserted slowing down into his routine. He says that he has moments each day of gratitude and happiness, and these joyful moments have been strung together in a beautiful tapestry of great weeks, months, and years.

The irony is that a lot of the busiest people forget that if you prioritize moments of pleasure and enjoyment and slow down enough to have them, you'll actually *save* time in the long run and become even more productive.

In *The Happiness Advantage*, world-renowned psychologist Shawn Achor shares some amazing data that reveals that the happier and more in the moment we are, the more successful we'll be.

Happier, less stressed people

- Are much more likely to hit their professional and personal goals for the future
- Make more precise and skilled doctors, diagnosing 19 percent more accurately

- Land 50 percent more sales in marketing professions
- Perform better in academic examinations than unhappy students[1]

I understand why people would think that if they slow down and focus on happiness, they might lose their edge at work. But according to this study, that's not true. Happiness, slowing down, and living in the present moment will not get in the way of you accomplishing great things. On the contrary, they will actually help you achieve your dreams and enhance your performance.

I know what it's like to be busy. I have two businesses, four children, and a schedule that's full of events, international travel, and TV appearances. And now I'm writing this book, with a deadline to hit. This might very well be seen as a stressful life, but I can assure you it's not. I don't actually consider myself *busy*. I choose how to spend time and energy on all these endeavors. Choosing how requires slowing down. Slowing down brings clarity. I have time for myself and time for my family. I pick up my kids from school, make dinner, play games, and tell them stories before bed. I have time for nature, meditation, exercise, and relaxation. For me, these enjoyable, life-enriching investments are instrumental to my success and productivity in my professional career.

Like John, you don't have time to *not* slow down. Strategically slowing down is the answer to living your best life. As well as bringing much more genuine happiness into your life, the practices that you will learn in this book will foster personal power, a sense of purpose, foolproof efficiency in the face of an endless to-do list, and something we're all lacking nowadays: passion. It is a universal truth that slowing down is vital to rediscovering our passionate zest for life, the kind we once had as children.

You'll learn a lot during the course of this book. But if you take only one piece of advice away from the entire thing, remember this:

Prioritize bliss over busy.

Now I'll show you how.

Principle 1

SLOW MIND

> Do you have the patience to wait till
> your mud settles and the water is clear?
> Can you remain unmoving till the right
> action arises of itself?
>
> —Lao Tzu, Tao Te Ching, Verse 15

Have you noticed the incessant chatter in your mind? Of course you have! That inner voice that's been there for as long as you can remember? In this chapter, we officially introduce the two of you to one another and explore how you can live in harmony rather than chaos.

The dialogue in the mind can be like having a noisy, inconsiderate roommate who plays loud music, has guests over without asking, and at times won't let you fall asleep. It's like "Hey, I know you said you want to sleep, but remember what Carlos said to you in the meeting today? What a jerk, right? Oh, and don't forget about your taxes. I know they aren't due for another few months, but you should probably start worrying about them right now before falling asleep. Oh, and speaking of money, if the stock market crashes, you won't have any savings and you won't be able to quit your job and build up your own business and you will have to work and hang out with Carlos for eternity! Okay, sweet dreams."

Wait a second, roommate of the mind, who invited you?

It's time to slow all that noise in the mind way down. Our thoughts, and the quantity of them, can be steered in a slower, more conscious, more pleasant direction. That's what you will learn in this chapter.

"Don't believe all the thoughts in your head," a teacher once told me. I want to take a moment to ask you to consider this: the thoughts in your head *aren't the real you*. They're not your identity. From a psychological standpoint, it's understood that thoughts can be influenced by a variety of factors, including your cultural and family upbringing, societal influences, personal experiences, and subconscious processes. Many thoughts can be seen as arising from the collective knowledge and experiences we've been exposed to rather than being solely "ours." Basically, when we overthink, our brains are just doing their weird and wonderful thing. We all know what it's like to have lightning-fast scripts running through our psyche, so most of us would agree that a lot of the time, our thoughts are neither authentic nor productive. At best, it's annoying to have a mind that races without our conscious consent. At worst, it can lead to extreme stress and other mental health issues.

Stress

Your Modern-Day Inheritance

Stress has won the award for the most widely experienced buzzword of our time.

It shows up everywhere: in magazines, on the radio, on news channels, and all over social media. It can be found lingering in the doctor's room, at the office, and in your own home. If you're not stressed right now, someone close to you probably is. You can rarely make it through a single day without stress creeping in with a surprising "Boo!"

But what is it, exactly? Stress is a combo of the emotional and physiological reactions that come about when an individual perceives a situation as either demanding or threatening. This leads to strain or doubt in their coping capabilities. This phenomenon constitutes a multifaceted psychosomatic response. In plain English, it's like your brain's way of saying, "Quick! Fight against the danger! Or if you can't do that, flee and get AWAY!" In reality, however, what most circumstances call for is to slow down and get out of the stress state so we can actually deal with the situation at hand.

In our modern world, life has become ever more fast-paced and increasingly complex. Combine speed, pressure, and complexity, and boom, you've got a breeding ground for stress. Even with our advances in technology and our modern environment, our bodies are still very primal, operating on the same cycles and rhythms as they have for hundreds of thousands of years. It's no wonder that balance is so difficult to achieve when we push ourselves in so many unnatural ways. We're just not built for doing a hundred things at once. And we're certainly not built to be under the iron fist of stress over extended periods of time while trying to survive in a concrete jungle. That's why it makes us so sick. (More on that later.)

This lightning-fast lifestyle leaves millions too depleted to nourish themselves psychologically, get sufficient exercise, do relaxation practices, or even spend quality time with other human beings. We're wired for connection, yet our worldly responsibilities often get in the way of our spending time with the people who make our lives worth living. This energy-depleting way of life and the chronic stress that comes with it can lead to a host of serious physical and psychological ailments. Cutting-edge medical research, as well as research dating back to the 1990s, estimated that up to 90 percent of serious illnesses and diseases are brought about by stress.[1] Let's face it, the number is probably higher now.

> **QUICK MYTH:** Regular stress is an inevitable part of life, so toughen up. You should be able to handle it!
>
> **SLOW REALITY:** Stress, when experienced chronically, is responsible for many serious illnesses. Bringing slowness to the mind and prioritizing your well-being will safeguard your brain and body, and therefore your life, against deterioration. Stress must be faced with a level of seriousness, just as physical illnesses are.

Are You Stressed?

Stress is dangerous. At its worst, stress can be a cause of death for human beings. It doesn't get more serious than that. At a milder level, it causes premature aging and a host of preventable diseases.

At best, stress causes immediate, very unpleasant feelings in the mind and body. And that's a kind of "best" you want to avoid. Take a moment to scan this list of symptoms of stress and identify any that you may have experienced in the past or that you're experiencing on a regular basis.

Do you ever get any of these physical signs of stress in your *body*?

- Tight muscles and body aches
- Fatigue
- Shallow, short breathing
- Chest tightness
- Rapid pulse
- Heartburn
- Indigestion
- Diarrhea
- Constipation
- Dry mouth and throat

- Excessive sweating
- Cold hands/feet
- Skin irritation
- Lowered libido
- Gut and stomach cramps
- Loss of appetite
- Insomnia
- Panic attacks
- Changes in your menstrual cycle if you have periods[1]

Do you ever get any of these psychological signs of stress in your *mind and mood?*

- Intrusive and racing thoughts
- Frustration, irritability, and anger
- Impatience and low tolerance
- Worry and anxiety
- Sadness or depression
- Tearfulness
- Insecurity
- Emotional instability
- Memory lapses, difficulty concentrating
- Indecision
- Loss of a sense of humor
- Loss of empathy and generosity
- Increased desire to consume alcohol and drugs
- Cravings for high-sugar, high-fat foods

- Lack of interest in life
- Feeling neglected or lonely[2]

I'm willing to bet that you have experienced one, more, or many of these symptoms on a recurrent basis. Very few people get through life unscathed by stress.

It's sad that this acute mental strain robs so many people of life's pleasures, and it's concerning that these symptoms have now become "normal." According to The American Institute of Stress,

- 33 percent of people report suffering regularly from extreme stress
- 48 percent of people can't sleep properly because of stress
- 73 percent of people see major impacts on their mental health caused by stress
- 77 percent of people experience stress that directly affects their physical health

And for varying reasons, the souls who suffer the most extreme levels of stress happen to be women, single parents, and ethnic minorities.[3]

Many of these physical and mental issues, it could be argued, arise not only from stress itself but from the way we handle it. The steady rise of addictions, drug and alcohol use, unhealthy, abusive relationships, and choosing entertainment over a good night's sleep (name-dropping my guilty pleasure of choice that rhymes with "Vetfix") can't have helped the situation. And once we have a physical or mental illness, we may well choose to numb the pain with even more unhealthy choices, such as comfort eating, splurging, toxic, unfulfilling casual sex, drug use, and generally reckless behavior.

We respond to stress in detrimental ways because we lack resources. And going to the doctor's office about it, nine times out of ten, will only get you a packet of Prozac or Valium thrown in your face, which opens a Pandora's box of side effects. (I'm not saying that anxiety and depression shouldn't be treated with medication; however, I argue that these drugs shouldn't be used lightly and without trying more holistic approaches first/alongside them.)

The results are in. Stress is the most silent, subtle pandemic of the twenty-first century. Worse still, this form of suffering has been globally accepted as part and parcel of the everyday. But just because it's normal doesn't mean it should be. And just because you've already had your fair share of it doesn't mean you should live with the pain of stress long-term. The good news is that you'll already be safeguarding yourself against a buildup of stress-related issues by practicing the Slow Method principles. Meditation, mindfulness, exercise, and healthy relating have been proven time and time again to reduce even the most extreme forms of stress.[4]

Contrary to what you may be feeling right now (because I've probably alarmed you), stress isn't all bad. It has one pretty useful benefit if relied upon in short-term, dramatic scenarios.

The Bear and the Big Silver Lining of Stress

Too much stress can be deadly, as we now know. But experiencing absolutely none of it can be deadly too.

The stress response evolved for a very good reason—to protect you from danger. I became all too familiar with this response early in my life. On my thirteenth birthday, my father took me to Alaska, a sort of initiation into manhood, an adventure into the wild. On our second day in the bush, we were hiking along a beautiful trail next to a river, watching the salmon jump upward toward the edge of a waterfall. As we stopped to admire the spectacular scene, a huge grizzly bear unexpectedly burst out of the bushes and trees and onto the trail a mere four feet in front of us. The bear was twice as tall as I was. I froze. To this day, I remember how suddenly dry my mouth became and how dramatically hard my heart was beating. I'm sure the bear could see it drumming through my waders!

At that precise moment, my body was basically giving me a choice—I could put up my dukes and have a wrestling match with my furry opponent, or I could find the quickest way to escape. This is known as the "fight-or-flight response." ACTH (the adrenocorticotropic hormone) was released into my bloodstream, and my adrenal glands immediately went to work to produce a huge amount of adrenaline and cortisol. My blood pressure rose dramatically, and my breathing rate amplified rapidly; my lungs wanted as much oxygen as they could handle so I could make a run for it if I chose to. My blood was then directed away from my skin and internal organs and sent to my brain and skeletal muscles. All of my muscles tensed up to make me temporarily stronger in case I chose to fight the bear. My blood cells rearranged their structuring so as to cause them to clot faster, just in case the bear actually caught me and tossed me around like a doll. This would, in turn, repair the near-fatal damage inflicted on my arteries as swiftly as possible.

Simultaneously, my pupils dilated, temporarily gifting me with better vision (not so necessary, as the one-thousand-pound grizzly was just four feet away). My liver then converted my glycogen stores into glucose, which teamed up with all my free fatty acids to supply me with an immediate burst of energy to fuel the attack or, in this case, my getaway. In a nutshell, my well-justified stress response caused a lot to happen.

The Alaskan fishermen of old and new always give the same advice: do not run if you come face-to-face with a bear. But I was a kid, and I thought I was going to die, so before I knew it, my mind had gone completely blank and my legs had sped off from under me like those of a roadrunner. My dad and I found ourselves sprinting down the trail and then scrambling up a tree faster than the local squirrels. Lucky for us, the bear was much more interested in the salmon jumping up the waterfall. We made that tree our home until the bear was well out of sight.

Under these circumstances, the fight-or-flight response of my younger self was totally appropriate. This primal bodily reaction served the cave dwellers throughout the Stone Age, Bronze Age, and Iron Age—and it worked like a charm. In fact, it's seen us through every stage of human evolution. And we still need this response just in case we happen to come face-to-face with a grizzly in our local national park, as my dad and I did. This reaction, however, should have to kick in only rarely—once in a blue moon for the modern individual living in the twenty-first century.

Yet, as a "modern man," I have experienced the exact same stress response from behind the wheel of my car and from behind my computer screen showing me an unpleasant email. Unfortunately, it seems that our bodies have not caught up with our environmental evolution. To our bodies, we're still living in the wild, and an office presentation is a lioness in disguise, just as much as our baby's cry is akin to the howl of a hungry wolf who's just about to pounce through the open cave door. Our bodies do not know the difference between the perils of the natural world and the stress that our modern life brings with it as collateral damage. In today's modern jungle, things like public speaking, a disgruntled spouse, difficult clients, deadlines, debts to be paid, and child-rearing, while not life-threatening, cause the same response as if they were. They release the same bombardment of stress hormones into the body.

Our body isn't just reacting; it's *overreacting*. And repeatedly triggering this fight-or-flight response wears it down. The mind swiftly follows this breakdown, as the pent-up stress has nowhere to go but *deeper in*. At least when a truly dangerous situation is at hand, this stress response has an outlet to express itself immediately. We either use up the energy to run for our lives or use every ounce of strength to fight off our opponent. The stress hormones don't stay in our body, and our system calms itself down relatively quickly when it's all over. But when it comes to today's stressful scenarios, nine times out of ten, we suffer in stillness and silence, like caged tigers. The stress stays in our bodies and minds. Over time, this type of stress becomes chronic and eventually can make us sick. This all makes sense, even to the most cynical of us, when it comes to the mind-body connection. A machine that constantly runs on overdrive without resetting itself is bound to crash and burn out.

Bottom line: keep your stress response only if you're face-to-face with a bear or an oncoming truck on the road you're crossing or a violent thief on the street corner. It'll save you. But it's high time to ditch it in all other areas of your life where it's become chronic.

Where do you start?

First aid.

Exercise #1: First Aid for Stress: Primal Shaking

The first need is for first aid. It's all well and good telling you to sit down and meditate (and trust me, I will), but if stress has already set in, wreaking havoc on your body, you need an immediate physical outlet for it. Just like zebras, polar bears, dogs, cats, and the myriad of other animals all discharge their stress response by shaking.[1] And shaking is not just for our furry friends; you will see athletes, performers, and Olympians shake before an event. Shaking transforms stress into vitality, tightness and tension into peak performance. Peak performance should be for all of us. If you want to bring your best energy forward and into your everyday life, do some shaking.

Take a moment to pause and notice any stress in your body. Where are you feeling it? What symptoms are you experiencing? If you're not stressed right now (good for you, by the way), imagine if someone asked you, "Where do you usually carry stress in your body?" Where would you point? Once you've clarified the area, whether it's your stomach, throat, jaw, head, or anywhere else in the body, you're ready to go.

Take a deep breath, and as you exhale, imagine blowing out the tension the stress has caused. Take another deep breath. This time, on the exhale, begin shaking your entire body. Bounce into your legs, relax your shoulders, pump your hands by relaxing your wrists, release the back of the head (cranial base), and allow that shaking to move through your spine. In Qi Gong, this is called "activating the five pumps." Do it for two to five minutes.

You may feel a bit silly at first, but this exercise is anything but stupid. You're giving your body, the primal animal beneath your skin, permission to shake off excess stress that you no longer need. Do whatever you need to do to get into the mood. Use your mind to bring forth the stressful situation so you can shake the poison out. Sigh loudly. Put on some dance music and let it all out. Keep breathing and shaking as strongly as you feel until the stress leaves your body.

Now stand or sit still and return to your breath. Return to slowness. Return to your center. Sense a light buzzing or tingling in your hands and fingers. Feel warmth and relaxation moving through your spine and nervous system. Practice slow breathing. Soak up the relaxation. Soak up the new, clean Qi.

Mindfulness

The Number-One Enemy of Stress

Now that you know how to perform shaky first aid on yourself once the stress has struck, it's time to learn some prevention techniques. It's time to cultivate the kryptonite of your stress. It's time to open a big ol' can of mindfulness.

"Mindfulness" happens to be a very popular buzzword, just like stress. But this one is widely misunderstood. To begin with, mindfulness is the opposite of "mind-fullness" (with a double "l"). You don't need me to tell you what it's like to have your mind . . . full. Full of doubts, worry, overwhelm, critical thoughts, fantasies about the future, and painful memories from the past. It's how the mind naturally rolls, so don't be too hard on yourself if you currently have a mind that's on overdrive, aka the "monkey mind."

We're hardwired to think on overdrive because, quite simply, it's how the human race survived for so long. The saber-toothed tiger had its, you guessed it, teeth. So did the shark, as it still strikes fear into the fishy hearts of millions today. The mammoth had its size and its strength. The primordial rodents had their smallness and scrappiness and could dive into tiny holes to shelter from natural catastrophes. Sapiens had, for as long as we can tell, the *mind*.

And *Homo sapiens* (that's us) triumphed over the Neanderthals (another type of prehistoric human being) for this reason. *We were smarter.* We could use the mind to predict future scenarios by remembering past circumstances.

That was our savior. We'd use our brilliant minds to plan, strategize, count, connect, and avoid danger way in advance. We were problem-solving machines, and no other creature on planet Earth could say the same for itself. You could say that, if nothing else, we had Big Brain Energy, and we used it to win at life and the game of evolution. It was all about survival of the fittest, and we were as fit as could be.

Because survival was the goal, our minds adapted to ensure that happened. But nowadays, our main goal in life has changed. We want more than just to survive—we want to *thrive*. We now, deep in our hearts, want happiness in life. We want to experience and give love. We want to live in a state of peace and balance. We want to make the world a better place. And that's great. The only problem is that the untrained mind will struggle to get there due to its primal programming and its infestation of ANTs.

ANTs (automatic negative thoughts) produce a constant, subtle undercurrent of anxiety. If we remain in this state long-term, this subtle anxiety will begin to flare up into stress when triggered by whichever stimulus happens to crop up. And if we stay stressed, it will eventually cause all of the nasty symptoms that were outlined earlier. To prevent stress from rearing its head in the first place, we must turn to the archnemesis of mental disorder, which is . . .

Mindfulness.

Simple, yet so effective. Mindfulness is the art of paying attention. It consists of slowing down the thinking mind and connecting to the present moment: the only moment we can possibly find happiness in. But the consequences of engaging in this practice are astronomically beneficial for our mental health. Mindfulness is not for the few. Mindfulness is for the masses. And we need it now more than ever.

> **QUICK MYTH:** The goal of life, just as it was thousands of years ago, is to survive. It's survival of the fittest! And stress will help us triumph.
>
> **SLOW REALITY:** While survival is still incredibly important, it is not the only goal of life. As an evolved species, we have a new goal: to thrive. And chronic stress holds us back from health, happiness, and bliss.

What does a mindful person look like? Well, for starters, you don't have to be from the Buddhist territories of Asia, where mindfulness has many of its original roots. You don't have to wear robes or continually exude an expression of peace. A mindful person is simply one who is actually *here* and *now*. They live their *actual* lives, not the one that exists solely in their heads. As a result, anxiety and stress are not commonplace. But it's an art to master. The mind is hardwired to overthink to avoid pain and pursue pleasure and therefore to be preoccupied with worry about what might happen or why something already did. This is the opposite of mindfulness.

So how do we practice mindfulness from a place of chaos? This has been a timeless inquiry of the mystics of Eastern traditions of meditation as well as Western psychologists, and that's what you will learn in this chapter.

Switch on your kettle. Things are about to get hot.

Welcome to the Mindful Tea Shop

Before I share the mindful tea ritual with you (to start training your mindfulness muscles tomorrow morning), let me tell you the story of a man I once met in a tea store in California.

On a rare occasion, we meet someone who embodies mindfulness, who is so eminently *here and now* that just being around them alters our experience of the moment. These people seem to radiate Technicolor tranquility. They emanate profound stability. Rather than succumb to a state of constant distraction—so easy in today's world of technological overload—they remain calm, present, and endlessly curious about the present moment.

I lived and worked near one of these rare individuals. He owned a tea shop, and unlike the cafés scattered on every corner, this tea shop didn't allow the use of cell phones or computers. There was no Wi-Fi, and he was proud of that. The instant you walked into that tea house, there was a palpable shift for the better in your state of mind.

I walked in one morning and greeted David, the owner, with a simple "Good morning. How are you?" He looked at me and responded with one word: "Fascinated." I smiled at his unique response. We are asked how we are multiple times a day, but very few of us answer truthfully and mindfully.

He smiled at me and turned his attention out the window toward the old birch tree outside, watching the breeze dance through the branches and leaves for a moment. He nodded to himself. Yes, he definitely seemed fascinated. He then held my gaze, just for a second, before asking me for my order. In this brief encounter, David had somehow managed to grasp my attention and stabilize it beneath the surface of my ordinary thinking mind. Everything became more alive and more colorful, the light through the trees sparkled brighter, and the sound of footsteps going by was almost melodic. It was as if the window of my awareness had been wiped clean.

With my cup of pu-erh tea steaming gently in front of me, I drank it slowly and mindfully over many moments. Pu-erh, a distinctive tea from the Yunnan Province of China, provides no anxiety-producing buzz. Instead, it is excellent for brain health and for the nervous system. Just the smell of it made me feel more relaxed, and its earthy taste grounded me even more. I don't know how long I was there that Sunday. It was the most special tea-drinking experience I'd ever had.

Being fully awake and conscious in the moment is always a fascinating experience. And the wonderful thing is that you can tap into the magic at any time. This is the very best way to experience life—in a state of mindfulness. Beneath our seemingly ordinary surroundings lies a world of captivating phenomena. From that day onward, I made a small yet powerful pledge to drink my tea differently.

Exercise #2: The Mindful Tea Ritual

Here's a simple exercise for you to try.

Make yourself a cup of tea (or coffee if you prefer. I'm a huge tea fan, and preparing the loose leaves in a teapot really hits the spot for me. But you do you).

Prepare it slowly and mindfully, and try not to be on your phone at the same time or listening to a podcast or loud music with lyrics. Once your beverage of choice is prepared, drink it slowly without doing anything else.

That's it.

This may well feel alien to a lot of people since we're used to downing our morning tea or coffee as quickly as possible to caffeinate ourselves without delay. This time, we're doing it differently. Slow down, feel into the experience, and take the time to be in the moment.

Take five minutes to smell, feel, and sip with full awareness. Notice the texture, taste, and temperature in your mouth. Follow the comforting sensation down the throat and into the belly. Take a deep breath, and then do it again. Notice how you feel throughout the process.

If you don't have ten minutes (and if this is you, consider waking up a tiny bit early to give yourself the gift of not having to rush), do the mindful tea ritual with just the first sip. This small act of mindfulness will encourage many more moments throughout your day. It will take you from living life on automatic to living life *awake*. As the Buddhist monk Thich Nhat Hanh wrote many years ago, "Drink your tea slowly and reverently, as if it is the axis on which the earth revolves—slowly, evenly, without rushing towards the future. Live the actual moment. Only this moment is life."

Autopilot and the Drunken Teenage Monkey

Helen did not drink her tea slowly.

I first met Helen in a Qi Gong workshop I was teaching back in 2011, and she was the least mindful person I believe I've ever met. Don't get me wrong; she was a very nice woman, but being around anyone who hasn't trained their mind into some kind of basic submission can be a little challenging even for the best of us. She had lots of questions that she catapulted into the middle of my lectures and even threw into the middle of a silent meditation. She had an abundance of contrasting, seemingly unrelated thoughts running through her mind, and she wasn't afraid to share them with anyone at any time, at lightning speed, in any depth of detail.

I'd be all "Take a deep breath and relax. Imagine sitting on a beautiful beach, sun setting softly into the hor—" and Helen would blurt out, "What color is the water, exactly?"

She also had many tales to tell. If someone else shared an intimate story, as opposed to listening, she'd butt in with a frequent interjection about her own life: "Oh, well here's what happened to me this one time . . ." followed by an unrelated personal anecdote. Many students in the class found it difficult to focus, and I noticed they were beginning to get agitated by her constant disruptions.

On the second day, I took Helen aside and asked her if she could hold questions and comments until after the sessions or the appropriate times. She was taken aback. When I told her that I appreciated her spirit and enthusiasm, but her interruptions were bothering the group, she was clearly upset. She didn't realize that she had disrupted the group so much. She said she was sorry, but she just couldn't help it. She felt bottled up most of the time, and it felt freeing to spill out the hyperactivity in her brain to a listening ear. Her mind never stopped. And it wasn't robbing just her of her inner peace but everyone around her too.

She had a classic case of the monkey mind, an overactive, untrained mind that is uncomfortably out of control.

(I'd like to note here that there is a difference between experiencing the monkey mind and being neurodivergent, with, say, attention-deficit/hyperactivity disorder [ADHD]. This is a condition that I'm by no means "calling out" here; rather, I'm referring to the untrained, overactive mind that can be rewired with meditation and mindfulness exercises over time.)

I felt for her. Like Helen, many of us have a hard time slowing down the mind and correcting the less-than-ideal behavior that a quick thought-stream causes. This seemingly uncontrollable mental flow is known in Chinese culture as the monkey mind, translated from Cantonese as an "internal teenage primate who has become drunken on stolen liquor."

I find this definition hilarious. So let me introduce you to that annoying roommate you've had in your head all these years—a tipsy adolescent monkey! Because it's not just Helen who has one; you do too. It's just that Helen's was probably a little more out of hand than yours.

I don't say this to offend your psyche. After all, it's a miracle thousands upon thousands of years in the making, with about a hundred billion neurons, each firing and wiring with thousands of other neurons.[1] To say it's an impressive evolutionary machine would be a huge understatement.

But with all due respect to this magnificent design, it tends to get pretty out of control, and we're still learning how to use it. The conditioned mind is often agitated and out of tune with reality, trained to stay asleep, nestled between the lines of internalized stories about ourselves and others. Admit it—it also has a comically entitled attitude. Just take a few moments today to examine the contents of your mind. If you're like most people, the mind will be complaining about someone or some situation, drumming up memories from the past (for your joy or despair), or fabricating video footage of upcoming stressful situations.

In addition, the thinking mind, at least most of the time, convinces us that we "should" be some place other than where we actually are. It complains that "this" shouldn't be happening, and it "wouldn't" be happening if only you'd done "that" differently. It's the greatest expert on the planet on *shoulda coulda woulda*.

Once, while teaching Qi Gong on the East Coast, I was tasked with driving from Vermont to Dartmouth College in New Hampshire. As I was meandering through the mountains, the sky opened up, and it started to rain *hard*. A deluge of water poured down from the heavens unlike anything I'd ever seen before. My windshield wipers couldn't even keep up with the liquid avalanche. As I approached a bridge along the mountain road, there was a detour sign. Apparently, the bridge had been washed away by the barrage of water. Up through the mountains I went, following the detour signs, until . . . no more signs. When I looked on my phone for GPS directions, there was no signal. I was completely lost.

I finally saw a couple of teenagers sitting on the porch of a beautiful countryside house beside an elderly man who I assumed was their grandfather. I was grateful to see them. I pulled over, pulled my jacket over my head, and stepped into the downpour to ask how to get to Dartmouth College in New Hampshire. The grandfather screwed up his brow in confusion and judgment and shouted, "New Hampshire? You really shouldn't be starting off from here!"

Yes, perhaps I shouldn't have been starting from there, but that's where I was. Where else could I start from? Partaking in the *shoulda coulda woulda* game wasn't going to help me get to my destination and get dry any quicker. What I needed was to be mindful, accept where I was, and get some direction on how to take the next step.

That's why so many spiritual traditions and practices teach us to be present. Relax into the moment. Gather your resources. And begin the journey from the only place you can: right here.

The grandpa finally begrudgingly gave me his sage advice after realizing that, unfortunately, I didn't have the skill to teleport myself down the mountain. He pointed me in the direction of the nearest highway.

So how exactly do we go about "gathering our resources"? How do we train the drunken monkey? You guessed it. It starts with radical acceptance of the present moment and a decision to embrace mindfulness. You already have one exercise: bringing mindfulness into your mornings with the tea ritual. But when it comes to truly training yourself to achieve a mindful human status, meditation is what will get you there. If you're new to meditation, don't worry. Or, in fact, *do* worry, because . . .

If You Can Worry, You Can Meditate

The difference between living a deeply satisfying life and one fraught with anxiety is often just one simple decision: the decision to train the monkey mind to be more present through meditation. This, however, is easier said than done, especially for those who struggle with generalized anxiety, rumination, depression, and future-based thinking when they sit down to meditate. For those with neurodiversity, meditation can also be very challenging. However, a wandering mind, distraction, and frustration are all completely normal for newbies to meditation, no matter how their brains are wired. It's even normal for experienced meditators to lose concentration and levels of mindfulness depending on how they approach their meditation cushion. In this case, as opposed to trying to force a currently square peg into a round hole, you can use anxiety as a launchpad to a more positive, joyful experience.

When I started getting into the art of Zen, I brought a friend to a meditation class. I'll always remember that session. He, like me, had a troubled, racing mind. As the teacher began guiding us through the meditation, my friend, face red from embarrassment, raised his hand and said, "I really can't meditate, sorry. My mind simply won't be quiet. I'll just let myself out."

As my friend prepared to leave, the teacher asked him, "Do you know how to worry?"

"Of course," my friend replied with a curious tone.

"Then you can meditate," said the teacher.

He explained that when we worry, we are meditating on what we *don't* want to happen. Meditation can be a simple flip of the same logic, a decision to pay attention to what we *do* want instead. An interesting theory is that, technically, we are all meditating most of the time. Watching TV can be a meditation, as your attention is focused on one thing (that is, of course, if you're not simultaneously on your phone and working on a project while cutting your nails). TV is an unconscious meditation, feeding your mind something to focus on. So is social media with its incessant barrage of new mind snacks to consume. Your mind is focused, concentrated, absorbed . . . these qualities cover many aspects of meditation, but they're just practiced unusefully.

As long as you're focused on one main activity, you're meditating on that activity. Traditional meditation, then, is just stripping it all to the bare bones of awareness. From this space we can observe the mind, get to know it, and give it a workout. Meditation is like your mind's local gym; you give the mind a good stretch and strengthening workout. Meditation stretches the mind to stay present without wandering and strengthens the mind by training it to concentrate.

Meditation is worry turned upside down. If you've found yourself sitting alone, fretting about your upcoming day, turn that worry on its head. Instead of focusing on what might go wrong, ask yourself a better question. Think of the opposite of that worry. If you are concerned about your upcoming day, do a little Aikido mind move and redirect the energy to what you want. Ask yourself, "What could go amazingly well today?"

Take it further, imagining how you would like to feel.

Picture the best-case scenario.

Imagine it now. You catch your train right on time. Your lunch with colleagues is delicious and satisfying. Your work goes swimmingly. Your movie night with your spouse goes romantically. You could feel contented all day long, despite the challenges that may arise. Use the momentum of your mind to catapult you into a whirlwind of radical positivity. It may feel a little unnatural at first, but once you get the hang of it, you'll be able to catch yourself before your negative, anxiety-ridden primate takes the wheel and ruins your morning.

A Thank-You Note

Let's take a moment to look at gratitude, an overlooked superpower when it comes to transforming the mindset from glass half empty to glass half full—and then from glass half full to glass overflowing!

Practicing gratitude involves bringing your attention to the gifts and blessings of your life, giving thanks for them, and celebrating them. It's a deliberate shift from focusing on negativity and absence to embracing positivity and abundance, allowing your inner voice to acknowledge this truth: you have much to be grateful for. Feelings of gratitude stem from two fundamental pieces of information that we process as we're feeling it: first, acknowledging the presence of the good things in our life and second, realizing that the origins of these blessings are, to some extent, external and "thanks" to other people, plain luck, and life circumstances.

Everything you own, eat, wear, use, and enjoy has other hard-working people behind it, whether they're textile specialists, farmers, builders, cooks, technicians, writers, or artists. And all the most beautiful, special moments of your life were facilitated by forces far beyond just "little old you." Gratitude reminds us that no human is an island and that all the good in our lives is a gift, not to be taken for granted.

Gratitude is the hidden key to joy. Happiness, after all, is what you get when you're in harmony with the present moment, yourself, and the circumstances in your life. Gratitude opens the door for this harmony. What's more, you can't possibly be immersed in appreciation and feel negative emotions at the same time.

How do we drop into a grateful state of mind? Step one is to *slow down*. True gratitude that's not forced or contrived happens organically and naturally when we slow down and drop into what we're receiving in the moment.

This happened to me recently with my daughter. I was on a business trip to Washington, DC. I was on *Good Morning DC* for my five minutes of airtime, teaching the hosts of the show how to clear stress and wake up with more energy.

Later that afternoon, my daughter and I took a bike tour of the national monuments. We rode around the Washington Monument, the Lincoln Memorial, the Martin Luther King, Jr. memorial, and many others. Toward the end of the tour, the sun was setting. We were overlooking the long pool, which was glowing red and orange as it reflected the afternoon sky. The clouds were glorious, filling the heavens like a mountain range of cotton balls. My daughter and I stood side by side looking at this incredible unfolding of nature that kept transforming with each passing moment.

Nature's display coaxed me into the moment. I was filled with gratitude. Appreciation bubbled forth from my heart into waves of deep thanks for the love I felt for my kids, the beauty of nature, my friends and family, my meaningful work . . . the joy of the moment unfurled through me with as much color as the ever-changing sky.

Gratitude can, of course, rise up within us naturally, as it did for me when I stood beside my beautiful daughter that afternoon in DC. But we can also integrate intentional gratitude into our day in strategic ways. For example, in all of our company meetings, we start with a round of gratitude. We go around the circle, whether it's live or on a video-call platform, asking each and every person what they are grateful for. It's light, pleasurable, sometimes funny, and sometimes inspiring and takes less than five minutes.

All of the world's ancient religions and spiritual texts teach the importance of gratitude, weaving it into their teachings and practices as a fundamental aspect of connecting with the divine and cultivating a deeper understanding of life's blessings. In various religious and spiritual traditions, gratitude is practiced through prayer, rituals, offerings, journaling, festivals, meditations, and a general attitude of gratitude toward whatever blessings are received. However, you don't have to be religious, or even deem yourself spiritual, to appreciate the power of gratitude and reap its benefits.

So what do you have to be grateful for right now? It can be something as simple as your health, your family, your job, your home, your memories, or the fact that you are breathing. When you wake up in the morning, you could give thanks for another opportunity to feel love, peace, and joy. When you go to bed at night, you could give thanks for everything that went well in your day: the steaming-hot mug of tea you enjoyed with your breakfast, the lovely music you listened to on your commute, the sunshine, the glorious walk you took at lunchtime, the cute message you received from your spouse, the paycheck that arrived in your account, the good company of your colleagues, the playtime with your children, the delicious food you had for dinner, that show that made you laugh out loud, and the book that accompanied you into the evening. We can even be grateful for the challenges we've faced in life and for every way in which they've helped us grow and become better people. There really is always something to be grateful for.

Being grateful also goes far beyond fleeting feelings of positivity. Robert A. Emmons and Robin Stern of the University of California, Davis and Yale University, respectively, conducted research on gratitude as a psychotherapeutic intervention for patients with mental health conditions and found that gratitude, above many other treatments, had a huge effect on psychological healing, including boosting alertness, enthusiasm, determination, attentiveness, and energy as well as reducing symptoms of physical pain and discomfort and, of course, helping with symptoms of depression.[1]

Despite its therapeutic potential, gratitude has been overlooked in most clinical contexts. It presents an untapped therapeutic resource that anyone can draw on. There are plenty of ways to practice. The most popular way by far is to keep a gratitude journal wherein you simply write a list of three to ten things you're grateful for. You could always add gratitude to an existing habit, for example, the mindful tea-drinking ritual we discussed earlier. This is a simple add-on gratitude practice I learned from a tea master named Dang Dang, a Buddhist monk who lived on a tea plantation in the mountains in China. The tea business had been in her family for hundreds of years, and her family grew the tea with love and reverence.

Dang Dang instructed us to hold our teacups in front of our hearts before we took our first sip. She encouraged us to bring awareness to this area of our bodies, to feel into the heart space. She then instructed us to give thanks to the farmers who had grown the tea. Then to give thanks to the plant that had grown the leaves. You could do the same with your coffee beans of choice.

Then, between mindful sips, you could allow yourself to reflect on the other blessings in your life.

That brings us to the next Slow Method exercise: a full gratitude meditation to provide you with the full range of benefits.

Exercise #3: Gratitude Meditation

Find a quiet and comfortable space where you won't be disturbed. Sit or lie down, and gently close your eyes. This is best practiced first thing in the morning or just before bed. Both is even better. Take a deep breath in through your nose, and exhale slowly through your mouth, releasing any tension. Begin by grounding yourself in the present moment. Feel the support of the surface beneath you. Notice the rhythm of your breath as you inhale and exhale, keeping you anchored in the now.

From a place of inner peace, shift your focus to what you're grateful for. Start with the small things—appreciate the air you are breathing, the beating of your heart, this moment in time. Recognize the everyday blessings that sustain you in your home, the little luxuries that many people don't have, like running water; a comfortable, safe place to sleep; food chilling in the fridge; heating or air conditioning;

washing facilities; clean clothes in the closet . . . Allow yourself to relish all the seemingly simple things that you're lucky enough to have.

Now bring to mind someone you're grateful for. It could be a friend, family member, mentor, or beloved pet. Picture their presence, recall their positive impact on your life, and feel a sense of gratitude emanating toward them. Take a moment to mentally express your thanks to this being. Silently share your appreciation for their role in your journey and the difference they've made to your life.

Redirect your gratitude inward. Reflect on your own qualities, strengths, and achievements. Acknowledge the challenges you've overcome and the progress you've made. Allow yourself to feel thankful for your growth and resilience.

Expand your gratitude to the world around you. Contemplate the beauty of nature, the interconnectedness of all living things, and the opportunities life offers. Develop an appreciation for the intricate tapestry of existence.

As you conclude, take a few deep breaths, marinating in warm feelings of appreciation. Inhale deeply, filling your lungs, and exhale slowly. Gently bring your awareness back to the present moment. Feel the ground beneath you and the gentle rise and fall of your breath.

Know that you can return to this practice whenever you need to reconnect with gratitude and joy. Before you open your eyes, silently express gratitude for this time you've dedicated to your well-being.

As you now know, not all meditation has something to do with "clearing your mind." On the contrary, you can work with the mind to give yourself a huge boost of peace and joy. From the gratitude practice we've just learned to positive projection, visualizations, and manifestation exercises, meditation can be as dynamic as you are. I could write a whole book on meditation, and there are many, but in the interests of this one, I'll walk you through one more very powerful meditation that trains the mind for slowness like no other. Nothing grants you a one-way ticket into the present moment more than the following meditative modality.

QUICK MYTH: Meditation is all about clearing your mind, and my mind is too busy for that. It's not for me.

SLOW REALITY: Anything can be a meditation as long as you're doing it with your full awareness. You are the master of your mind. Bring to your awareness something you appreciated about your day or your week. Think about something that you are looking forward to in the future. You did that. You moved your mind. That is meditation.

Mindfulness Meditation

Where Are You?

Once you have swept away some of your ANTs with the power of gratitude, sitting down to mindfully meditate in the traditional way won't feel so daunting. In fact, it will feel exhilarating.

When you slow down and tap into mindfulness, you realize where you actually are. Your mind wakes up from its thoughtful slumber, and the sweet clarity of the moment unfolds. We need this more than ever, especially if we're often heavy with emotions such as stress, anger, and sadness. These emotions, 99 percent of the time, arise within us and blow up due to turbulent thoughts and rumination, aka not being in the present moment. That's where the "Where Are You?" mindfulness meditation comes in.

Anyone can do this, anywhere and anytime. You can be alone, with others, in a peaceful atmosphere or an undesired chaotic whirlwind. This is a medicinal psychological exercise with no side effects and no end to its benefits. It is both the prevention of stress and the cure for it. Before I take you through it, let me tell you the story of the monk who gave it to me.

It was 2018, and I was sitting in a hotel room in northern China, interviewing a world-renowned Tibetan lama. He was a highly revered rock star in his country and had an entourage of monks by his side, tending to his every request. I felt honored to interview him. After introducing myself, I brought up the topic of mindfulness meditation and how popular it was becoming in the Western world. I asked him to explain the concept in his own words.

He looked at me and responded with a short sentence in Tibetan. The translator then offered the English translation to me: "Where are you?"

I paused. The translator continued, "He asked you the question, 'Where are you?'"

I smiled and responded, "Well, I'm here."

The monk responded again in Tibetan. The translator replied, "How do you know?"

I was taken aback by the simplicity of the question and the lama's piercing yet loving gaze. I felt a funny sensation come over me, as if the room had somehow become wider. It was as if my peripheral vision expanded. I didn't know how to respond in words, but I felt it in my bones. I was right there with him, totally at one with my surroundings. My mind quieted, and vast spaciousness entered into my awareness. The monk smiled knowingly.

This was mindfulness meditation.

"You are here. You were always here, even when you forgot and got very lost in the dream of your mind."

For the rest of the day, it was surprisingly hard not to be in the present. As the camera crew pushed me for plans for the upcoming week, I had to make a special effort to focus on the future. I was so present and rooted in the moment that I'd become fascinated by the here and now. Usually, it was difficult for me to stay in the present, but this time, it felt different. And this huge psychological change had come about due to the dazzling simplicity of one powerful question: "Where are you?"

The Tibetan monk further explained his mindfulness technique a day later, suggesting ways to expand on the question and coax the mind into the moment in deeper, more nuanced ways. Here is the meditation that he instructed me to follow daily (at least once formally but multiple times a day informally if needed to awaken me from the habit of anticipating the future and ruminating on the past). The beauty of this exercise is that it can be completed in just one minute or can be practiced for thirty minutes as a full practice if time allows.

Exercise #4: The "Where Am I?" Meditation

1. Take one deep breath, and with your eyes opened or closed, ask yourself aloud, "Where am I?"
2. Pause and take another deep breath. Even before you answer the question in your mind, chances are you're a little more present than before and the incessant merry-go-round of repetitive thinking has slowed a tiny bit. Respond in your mind, "I am here."
3. Sense and feel where "here" is. Pay attention. Listen. Notice the sounds in the room. See. Notice what surrounds you. Feel. Notice the sensations on the surface of your body. The chair, the floor, the clothes against your skin. Say again, "I am here." Be here now.
4. Now turn your attention inward. Feel the breath coming in through the nose and out through the mouth. Notice how the air passes through your windpipe to expand your chest and belly. Stay present with your breath.
5. Ask yourself again out loud, "Where am I?"
6. Respond, "I am here." You know you're here because you can feel it in your breath. You can't take a deep breath in the past. You can't take a real breath in the imaginary future. The breath, like peace and joy, can happen only in real time, right now.
7. Keep repeating the question and answer as you scan your body from the top of your head down to your face, neck, and

shoulders. "Where am I?" Scan down from your shoulders to your arms and then the tips of your fingers. "I am here." Scan down from your chest to your stomach and your gut, from the top of your spine to your tailbone. "Where am I?" Scan from your pelvis, glutes, and genitals to the tops of your thighs and down to your knees. "I am here." Scan down from your knees to your calves and shins, down to your ankles and feet, and all the way to the tips of your toes, letting tension melt from the muscles and bones. "Where am I?"

8. Feel your entire body in the space you're in. "I am here."

When you're ready, you can end your meditation with a big slow breath in and a very slow breath out through the nose. Return your focus to whatever you were doing before or whatever you're doing next with a newfound sense of mindfulness.

BONUS VIDEO MEDITATION: You can stream or download a free video version of this meditation if you go to qigo.ng/slow and select "Exercise #4."

Why Do You Want to Live Here, Anyway?

You're coming to the end of an entire chapter on the landscape of the mind. And every single word I have written can be summed up in one sentence, one piece of advice.

Be mindful and live in the present moment.

There are many compelling reasons to live here. And when I say "here," I mean *now*. Not in your head, as most people do, because living through a psychological lens of excessive thought is starkly different from actually living in the real world. Contrary to what your mind would have you think, the only place you can ever be is here and now. Even when you are thinking about the past or the future, you are thinking these thoughts in the present moment. Getting grounded in that fact helps clear the clutter of the mind and allows our consciousness to be rooted in reality.

From the moment, thinking about the past or imagining into the future can be done with clarity. Grounded in the moment, you connect to the choice maker in the mind rather than the habituated thought patterns. You can, in the moment, think about the past, choosing to conjure up memories of gratitude or even past sorrows. Being firmly rooted in the moment allows us, from a felt sense, to know that our past sorrows and disappointments contribute to our learning and growing.

Bliss. Joy. Peace. Happiness. Love. Serenity. Gratitude. Insight. Interest. Connection. All the good stuff is available only in the present. And subconsciously, we know this. In life, we are always secretly seeking to be in the here and now. We even create yearly rituals to facilitate easy integration into a pleasurable present. Think of Christmas, Thanksgiving, birthdays, Valentine's Day, Mother's and Father's Days, weddings, graduations, housewarmings, and New Year's. We set up a context where our attention will be heightened and focused in the present moment. It's not the event itself we are seeking; what we actually want is to be present, connected, and elevated in the moments of life.

As for a treasure hunter, these kinds of moments often need to be excavated. And you don't have to wait until the next celebration to feel all those blissful feelings that can be found in the now. They are always right underfoot. If we dig deeper, the present moment provides us with gems to polish and an abundance of joy to be revealed.

You can create your own daily rituals to facilitate present-moment awareness. And it doesn't always have to be meditation. Meditation trains the mind to be more aware. When you are more aware, you recognize, realize, and appreciate the gems of life moments.

For example, I've made a habit of watching as many sunsets as I can. I'm fortunate to live by the ocean, so my ritual includes a short walk to the beach, followed by the selection of the perfect spot and an investment of ten minutes to watch the golden semicircle of light cascade down over the horizon. There's something about this daily transition, where the fire of the sun meets the water of the ocean, that feels uplifting and cleansing beyond words. As the changing light paints pinks, oranges, blues, and purples across the sky, I feel something shift in my mind and body. All my senses heighten, and I begin to notice not just the visual beauty of the scene but also the symphony of sound around me: the waves drumming on the shore, the wind blowing through the instruments of the trees, and the birds singing in harmony above. I also notice the soft breeze caressing my arms and the back of my neck. I notice the last warm, comforting rays of sunlight illuminating my bare skin. It's often my favorite part of my day.

When you drop into the moment, *you wake up.*

For each of us, there are certain environments and certain people that allow us to come alive more fully. For me, among many others, one of those is sunsets.

What about you?

> **QUICK MYTH:** In today's fast-paced reality, we must embrace constant forward thinking and live more in the future.
>
> **SLOW REALITY:** In order to live life fully, we must connect with the present moment more often. Contentment, joy, and peace are often only a flicker of attention away. Bring the mind into the moment, relax, and breathe.

Exercise #5: Make Your Mindfulness List

What situations bring you into the present moment? What people in your life make you feel more present? Grab your journal and make a list now. Then make a commitment to do more of what's on your list or be around those people more.

Example Mindfulness List:

- Sunsets
- Sunrises
- Walks in my local park
- Being intimate with my partner
- Traveling
- Being with [INSERT FRIENDS]
- Playing with my child
- Eating at great restaurants

- Meditating
- Doing Qi Gong
- Practicing Tai Chi
- Listening to my favorite music
- Breathwork
- Massages
- Yoga
- Reading in bed with hot chocolate
- Watching new movies at the theater
- Swimming in the sea
- Cold-water therapy
- Dancing
- Shopping
- Hiking
- Writing
- Sipping a delicious cup of tea

Once you're done, make a commitment to engage in these mindfulness-inducing activities more often. There's no time like the present moment, so why not grab your calendar now? When can you make time for these moments for the remainder of this week?

Eckhart Tolle said, "Realize deeply that the present moment is all you ever have."[1] And if that's true, as I believe it is, then it's time for us to change the way we live. It's time to train the drunken teenage monkey, slow down, and become present in the natural magic that is in and all around us.

Your Mind Is a Garden

As we come to the end of Principle 1, I will leave you with this popular saying (origin unknown, though often incorrectly attributed to the nineteenth-century English poet William Wordsworth): *Your mind is a garden; your thoughts are the seeds. You can grow flowers, or you can grow weeds.*

The mind truly is a garden, and from now on, with the help of meditation and positive thinking, it's time to tend to it.

Cultivating a sound, healthy, unhurried mind is at first akin to tending to a messy landscape where every thought, idea, and emotion is a seed that can grow into something beautiful or unruly. Just as a gardener meticulously nurtures their plants of choice, we must take care to nurture our thoughts and therefore our inner peace, presence, resilience, and joy. We must take care to turn our focus toward constructive ideas and healthy habits that benefit our psychological landscapes.

Because it won't happen on its own. Remember, it's naturally full of ANTs. Just like a garden, the mind requires attention, care, and mindful cultivation over time to keep the critters and the weeds at bay. A good gardener must diligently remove weeds to ensure the health of their tender, growing flowers and allow them to flourish.

Of course, in both gardening and tending to the mind, setbacks are inevitable. Adverse weather can destroy the plants and disrupt their growth, and life's challenges can impact our mental state and the consistency of our slow practices. Yet just as a tough-as-nails landscaper adapts to changing conditions, we too can develop resilience in the face of adversity. By nurturing a strong foundation of positivity, gratitude, self-awareness, mindfulness, and meditation, we can weather life's storms with grace.

Once we have our garden of the mind blooming, we're ready to move on to the second Slow Principle.

It's about to get physical.

Principle 2

SLOW BODY

> Treat your body like a temple, not a woodshed.
> If you take good care of it, your body can take you
> wherever you want to go, with the power and strength
> and energy and vitality you will need to get there.
>
> —Jim Rohn

When it comes to our often aching, run-down, sleep-deprived, twenty-first-century bodies, something seems amiss. In general, we don't move our bodies enough. And when we do, we lug them around unconsciously—too quickly and without love. It's then that we risk developing illnesses or aggravating them further.

When Julia first started her Qi Gong class with me, she was not in a good way. She was suffering from chronic fatigue and debilitating pains in multiple areas of her body, and her relationship with herself was a rocky one. She felt that her body was failing her, and consequently, she was failing her body. For years, she locked herself away, feeling unable to pull herself out of the pit in which she found herself. She was referred to me by another student who had obtained substantial relief from fibromyalgia through mindful, slow movement. Julia was skeptical from the moment she walked through the door because over the previous five years, she had tried a variety of talking therapies without obtaining much relief.

I could tell that Julia had an agitated nervous system just by the way she spoke. She approached me quickly after our first class, red in the face. I noticed that her clothing was constricting her body, digging into the skin on her shoulders and nipping in her waist. An incessant stream of thought poured out before I could articulate the need for comfortable clothing. . . . "Thanks for the class, I feel a bit better, even though I still have pain, which I didn't expect to go away in the first class. My doctor recommended that I do some kind of movement, do you know Dr. Walker? I think her kids are in school with yours. Anyway, I've had chronic fatigue for years now, which nobody really knows anything about, but it's really debilitating. Some days I can't get out of the house. It's a good thing that I can see the beach from my balcony, otherwise, I'd be so bored . . ."

Julia, it seemed, was seriously in need of reading the "Slow Mind" chapter of this book, as her monkey mind was in full swing.

I smiled and listened before congratulating her for coming. I told her that the more time she dedicated to mindfully slowing down her body, the better she'd feel. As Julia continued attending class over the next three months, her overall demeanor slowly shifted each week. One evening, as I taught the class a slow-flowing movement called "Waving Hands Like Clouds," I caught a glimpse of Julia's wet cheeks from across the training hall. She continued the movement, silently and slowly breathing with tears pouring down her face. Her body was soft and moving with graceful ease, and she had a subtle smile playing around the corners of her mouth. I could almost see the healing happening.

I'm happy to share that Julia is now completely cleared of her chronic fatigue diagnosis. She feels she has more energy than she had when she was twenty-five years old and feels a sustained sense of relaxation throughout her daily life. By practicing slow movement, the body learns to move without tension. Often emotions are held and stored in the tissues of the body. As the body relaxes, emotional stress is released. When emotional stress is released, energy circulates in the body more efficiently. This explains Julia's reaction while practicing Qi Gong. This energy that circulates throughout the body is known as "Qi" in the East, and it's the same life-force energy that runs through all beings in the universe. It's the key to living a life full of health and vitality, and according to the ancient wisdom traditions, the best way to get in touch with it is to slow down.

Mindful movement has increasingly become popularized in the Western world with practices such as Yoga, Tai Qi, and my personal favorite, Qi Gong. Despite some modern twists like sweaty hot Vinyasa Yoga in luxury saunas for an astronomical price tag, these forms of exercise are all based on the ancient principles of slowing down, being mindful of your body mechanics, and circulating your system's internal energy.

Over the past thirty years, I have been fortunate to be able to teach slow, mindful movement to millions of people all over the world. What I've seen when people practice these slow arts has been truly revolutionary: when people consciously slow down the body, miracles happen. No wonder Qi Gong has been described as "the art of preventing illness and prolonging life" by so many Taoist masters.

As well as providing deeply therapeutic benefits for the practitioner, slow, controlled physical exercises such as Qi Gong can have a profound effect on performance and even, dare I say, a hangover.

In this chapter, you will learn how to slow down various functions and factors in your body. By slowing down your body, you slow down aging, prevent disease, increase energy, and calm the mind. After reading this sentence, did a little voice in your head say something like "Yeah, sign me up"? Well, it did for a New York City professional ballet dancer one Sunday morning.

The Surprising Physical Impact of a Slow Practice

I was hosting another Qi Gong workshop about an hour north of the city in the beautiful countryside by the Hudson River. The workshop was for beginners and focused on how to use Qi Gong and slow, smooth movements to get into the "flow state." This is very useful for dancers, professionals, retirees, therapists, and those participating in any other life performance. The turnout was great. Before we dove into the basics of Qi Gong, I wanted to get to know the participants a little better by asking their names and how they'd come across the ancient practice.

I nodded and smiled as the usual formal answers came flooding in, you know, the "I'm Angie and a friend of mine told me about you," "I'm Stuart and I Googled it," "I'm Donna and I saw you on TV" sort of thing. Short and sweet . . . until we came to the young, vibrant, and flamboyant ballet dancer, Kevin.

With an accent somewhere between a 1980s LA Valley girl and a New York City barista, Kevin shared his story: "You want to know how I discovered Qi Gong. Okay, well here it is. . . . So there I was, hungover as f*ck this one Sunday morning after one of those Saturday nights in New York, you know . . ." At this point, he winked at me. I noticed some of the well-mannered folks in the group squirming a little in their seats, unsure whether they should laugh or recoil. I stifled a laugh. "And anyway, I was like flicking through the TV channels,

I couldn't even move my body off the couch, I was seriously feeling like sh*t! So yeah, there I was surfing the stations, and suddenly I see this really handsome man on this random public television channel, standing on like a plank or something, in a RIVER, super cool, moving his body super slowly, like really, really slow, and I was like, 'Okay, what the f*ck is this?'"

He laughed and looked over at me. "And so I managed to peel my ass off the sofa and ended up doing the entire Qi Gongy routine with him in my jammies . . . and BAM! My headache was GONE! Like, *gone* gone! Qi Gong had totally cured my hangover, so yeah, that's why I'm here. Oh, and I'm a professional ballet dancer, and anything that helps me get into that flow zone is what I need."

This was one of the more colorful introductions I'd ever heard. I thanked Kevin for sharing, and we commenced the workshop. I continued working with Kevin for the months that followed, and he reported that he had not only discovered the "Holy Grail" of hangover cures but also begun to use Qi Gong as a warm-up before his ballets. He would practice the movements we had learned together to get into a calm, relaxed, optimal state for performing. Mindful movement of the physical body helped increase Kevin's longevity as a professional ballet dancer, and he carried on performing well after the typical retirement age. He thanked the Qi Gong–induced flow state for this. Kevin discovered that sometimes the key to peak performance, in work and in life, is, paradoxically, relaxation of the physical body.

I think we could all do with trying this out. After all, if we keep carrying tension and bracing ourselves against our lives, our bodies will eventually pay the price.

Relax

Your Plane Will Take Off Without Your Help

The plane was about to take off. I noticed that the woman sitting next to me was clearly nervous about flying. My first clue was the small bottle of vodka she was sneaking sips from as the plane slowly taxied down the runway.

As the plane turned to start its acceleration for takeoff, she gripped the armrests until her knuckles were white. As soon as the plane started to lift off the ground, she pulled up on her seat belt with significant force. She held her breath, scrunched up her face, and continued to pull up her seat belt. She looked like she was doing a heavy weightlifting session at the gym. I wanted to say, "Thank you for lifting the seat belt so hard; I'm sure it helped the plane take off," but refrained.

We all, in one way or another, attempt to lift the plane off the ground. I'll bet you've been a passenger in a car that's driving just a little too fast and pushed against the floor as if you were braking. We all struggle in vain as we attempt to influence the external world.

What is the plane in your life that you are trying to lift off the ground? Bring a situation to mind now. It could be as profound and painful as a family drama outside your influence or something as simple as a change in weather that's messed up your plans for the weekend. Perhaps unexpected traffic when you are trying to get somewhere in a timely manner.

As you think of whatever situation you feel resistance to, notice what happens to your body. Odds are you stiffened up. We tend to tighten our bodies when we feel out of control. We contract our muscles as a way to have influence, just like the woman who tried to lift the plane off the ground.

Our default way of attempting to control an external situation is to STOP, brace ourselves, hold our breath, and contract our muscles. But excessive contraction and tightening of the body maximizes mismanaged energy, which can drain us and limit the power that circulates through us. Imagine walking around all day contracting your arm muscles. After a short while, you would be thoroughly exhausted. That said, we all carry excess tension for most of the day. Tension in the neck and shoulders is common for many, especially those who work at desks. And if we carry it for too long, the muscles can actually forget how to relax. *We* forget how to relax. That's how tension becomes chronic.

That begs the question of whether this strain does any good. The answer is a very disappointing and resounding *no*. This excess tension doesn't make a blind bit of difference in the external world and does nothing except make you feel knotted up in your body. All this stress causes discomfort and dis-ease in the body. But as Kevin, the ballet dancer, came to learn, there's a better way.

Let Go of Control, and Go with the Flow

That's where physical relaxation comes in. Instead of going against the grain with resistance and pain, we can let go of control and enter a state of flow.

The definition of true "flow" is a far cry from the stereotypes surrounding the word. Going with the flow is not synonymous with living passively. Living in flow simply requires you to let go of that which you cannot control so you can channel your energy into what you can. "Flow" can simply be described as what happens when you relax, get out of your own way, and allow creative power to move through you.

In flow, you lose all sense of the passing of time, and it feels amazing to live and work in the flow state. The world's best martial artists, athletes, and performers all know that the secret to peak performance is flow. They know what the flow or the "zone" feels like and aspire to enter it before they take to their chosen arena. Watch an Olympian before an event, and you'll see them practicing all kinds of techniques. They shake, dance around, jump, slap themselves, wiggle, exhale fully, and inhale deeply. They are releasing stress, relaxing, and powering up. They are doing Qi Gong and don't even know it!

Flow, relaxation, and living in the zone aren't just for high-level performers. They're much-needed states of being for all of us. When we're in flow, the body and the mind lose track of the clock, which relieves psychological pressure. In this profound state of relaxation, connectedness, and focus, we're able to live, love, and contribute to society as our very best selves.

Psychologists Jeanne Nakamura and Mihaly Csíkszentmihályi describe it as a sensation of peaceful, intense concentration, where the only thoughts that arise are laser-focused on the experience at hand as opposed to themselves, therefore merging their actions and their awareness.[1]

If getting into the flow is the goal, the practice of Qi Gong is a time-honored practice of doing so. "Qi Gong" can be translated from Chinese medicine scriptures as something along the lines of "the practice of enhancing the energetic essence of the human body and mind" "the art of preventing disease," or "the mastery of life-force energy." It was born from some of the most respected healing and medical practices of Asia, and it's a practice I've dedicated most of my life to. Well refined over five thousand years of evolution, Qi Gong is one of the most ancient forms of therapeutic exercise and is the mother of practices like Tai Chi and many other branches of martial arts.

The ancient masters unlocked the sacred state of flow through Qi Gong, finding that slowing down bodily and mental activity allowed them to access a vault of health benefits without force. Moreover, the magic that is unleashed through this kind of movement meditation is strongly supported by modern science, from dramatic improvements in heart-health biomarkers to less risk of falling, from more strength and flexibility to increased levels of psychological well-being and even healthier personal relationships.[2] The perks of slowing down the body in this way are truly astonishing. Simply put, practices like Tai Chi and Qi Gong use the power of slowness to cultivate Qi (life-force energy), which improves your health as well as offering a fast pass to the flow state, an experience of superproductivity, power, and peace.

QUICK MYTH: In order to get what we want in life, we need to make it happen and use fast fell swoops of force to get there.

SLOW REALITY: Slowing down, relaxing, and feeling into the flow of the moment are the true keys to productivity and happiness.

Surfing into Flow

I was once talking to a professional surfer about the concept of flow. We were overlooking a huge cliff on a sunny day near Pleasure Point Beach, one of the best surfing spots in California. I asked him what he liked about surfing and why he'd chosen it as his career path.

He told me that surfing was a way of life for him. It wasn't just something he did; rather, it was *part* of him. He said that whenever he surfed a wave, there was no separation between him and the wave beneath him. They moved in unison. He went on to describe how there was a simplicity to life in that moment, with just his physical body and the wave existing. There were no thoughts, no worries, no expectations; there was only the flow.

In order for this to happen, all he had to do was relax and "let the surf take over." He described the rush of descending into the barrel of the wave, "like everything dissolves into continuity and time just stands still. Even though I can be zipping down the face of a huge wave at a crazy speed, to me, it all feels like everything is in slow motion."

This slowing-down perception is a classic description of flow state and peak performance. From this inner shift, the perception of the external world becomes clarified, and a harmonious relationship between you and the external environment is born. As he spoke about his passion, I couldn't help but notice the serene, deeply contented expression on his face. Every word he spoke was through a smile. And this makes sense. According to Mihaly Csíkszentmihályi (whom I mentioned earlier—he's an impressive expert on flow states, so if this topic interests you, try watching his 2004 TED Talk about it), flow states are the key to happiness, and the most resilient, influential people in the world regularly connect to flow.[1]

There is nothing more natural than flow for humans and nature alike. The ocean itself, waterfalls, streams, and running rivers express this truth. Take the river as an example: it moves down its mountain with intrinsic flow and power. Because of this, sheer strength is inherent within the river, and there's no need for force or tension. It is both soft and gentle, powerful and strong. Run your fingers through it, and it's soft. Try swimming the opposite way, against the current, and you'll feel its force.

The river finds the path of least resistance to avoid becoming blocked. It swims over rocks, swirls around boulders, and dives over cliffs without any struggle and without an ounce of stress. You have this water element within your physical body and possess the same intrinsic power.

Channeling Your Inner Bruce Lee

Empty your mind. Be formless, shapeless like water. Now you put water into a cup, it *becomes* the cup. Put it into a teapot, it *becomes* the teapot. Now water can flow or creep or drip or *crash*. Be water, my friend."[1]

Any Bruce Lee fans out there will probably recognize this world-famous quotation. Apart from sounding absolutely badass, especially in the dulcet tones of Bruce's accent, the passage contains a lot of wisdom.

First, around 60 percent of your body is made up of water.[2] And if you think of yourself as water with consciousness, you can appreciate that by nature, you need to move. Any body of water must be in some kind of flow in order to avoid stagnation, and your body is no different. Just look at the average office worker, who is required to sit in the same chair at a desk for hours a day—up to 69 percent of them end up developing neck and lower-back pain.[3]

Stress and a sedentary lifestyle block our flow of Qi energy, that which keeps us healthy and pain-free. Without knowing it, we end up blocking the circulation of energy that is meant to flow through us freely like water. Circulation is power. You can think of that energy as a form of currency, the life-giving tool we all use to get through our day, do the things we need to do for our work, love our families, and live life with passion and meaning.

When you tighten your body against the stresses of the world and remain unmoving, you create a dam in your body's river. And as we know, when water is walled off and trapped, stagnation ensues and gunk begins to build, taking vital nutrients from the water itself. It's like the ancient Qi Gong saying, "Flowing water doesn't get stagnant, and the hinges of an active door don't get rusty." This is true for our physical bodies too. Sitting is apparently the new smoking. Research has found that a scarcity of physical exercise has potential links to many health issues, particularly cardiovascular disease and the development of insulin resistance and therefore type 2 diabetes.[4]

So be like water, my friend. It's time to get up off your chair and move your a—

. . . arms.

There are a host of options to get your body into a relaxed sense of flow. But for now, let's start with the basic "Go Slow, Enter the Flow" Qi Gong Sequence. As every body is different, feel free to adjust this exercise, and all of the physical exercises in this book in ways that feel safe, fulfilling, and comfortable.

Exercise #6: The "Go Slow, Enter the Flow" Qi Gong Sequence

1. Stand with your feet shoulder-width apart with your knees just slightly bent.
2. Notice how your body feels. Sense where you might be holding tension or tightness, and physically relax those muscle groups.
3. Inhale and slowly raise your arms to shoulder height. Your elbows should be fairly straight. You can imagine that you have strings gently pulling your wrists upward. You should look like you're impersonating a chilled-out zombie.
4. Exhale and float your arms back down slowly.
5. Repeat these movements, inhaling your arms up and exhaling them down. As you practice this physical flow, keep your upper back, neck, and shoulders as relaxed as possible.
6. With each breath, see if you can relax even more.
7. Close your eyes. Think of your arms as the waves of the ocean, and feel the element of water within you.

8. Do this 10–20 times as a moving meditation. Be mindful of your breath, of the sensations in your body, and of the feeling of air moving through your fingers and across your arms.
9. Bring your arms to your sides. Relax. Now notice how your body feels.
10. Sense the feeling of lightness and relaxation moving through you. There might even be a feeling of electricity, tingling, and buzzing at your fingertips. This sensation is what was referred to as "Qi," the life-force energy, by all the greatest masters of the Eastern traditions.

With a bit of luck, this exercise has proved to you that by moving slowly and deliberately, you can feel both relaxed and energized at the same time. Slowing down, paradoxically, can give your body and mind more energy to do more of what you love. (And what you *have* to do but are procrastinating on, like your tax return.)

BONUS QI GONG ROUTINE: You can stream or download a free video version of this Qi Gong routine if you go to qigo.ng/slow and select "Exercise #6."

If You Are Forced to Sit on Your Butt All Day

Flow is served on a silver platter for surfers. It's a force that's there for the claiming for anyone in any profession that allows them to move and express themselves creatively, artistically, and musically. It's even there for those who have the freedom to remove themselves from the public eye to reconnect with their bodies in privacy. But what if you're literally paid to sit in the same chair?

If you work at a desk, it's entirely possible that even your trips to the bathroom are monitored, so for you, whipping out the Chinese flute CD and flowing in an elegant Qi Gong sequence like the one mentioned above in the middle of the day may well be too much to ask.

But you can always take a "Qi break." Get it? Like tea break, but with Qi . . . moving on.

So for those of you whose butts are glued to a chair for upward of eight hours per day, here's an exercise that you can carry out from your desk, all the while remaining seated if you need to. It's called "Spinal-Cord Breathing" and also has its roots in the ancient practice of Qi Gong. I mentioned a very alarming statistic in the last section about office workers and the shockingly high cases of backache due to a sedentary lifestyle. This will save you from that fate.

Exercise #7: Qi Break: Spinal-Cord Breathing

1. Sit up straight on the edge of your chair, with your spine free. This exercise can also be done standing if you have the opportunity.
2. As you take a deep breath in, reach your arms up to the sky, then imagine slowly pulling down an imaginary barbell weight to the tops of your shoulders. You want to encompass the classic weight-lifter pose, only your chest will be open and curling upward toward the sky. Bend your spine backward and look up at the ceiling to encourage an opening in the chest space.
3. As you exhale, curl your spine inward and bring your arms down, hands touching centrally in fists, all the way to your groin area so you can fold yourself into a little ball. Tense your glutes as you do this.
4. Inhale, and reach your arms up toward the sky again, opening up your chest, bending backward, and pulling down that imaginary barbell. Repeat this process of expansion and contraction for one minute or until you feel relief in your spine.

Combine Spinal-Cord Breathing and "Go Slow, Enter the Flow" to make the practice a little longer. Start with Spinal-Cord Breathing as a warm-up, then move to "Go Slow, Enter the Flow" as a slow-moving meditation. Go deeper by doing both movements for longer. Start with one minute of each and work your way up to five minutes of each for a combined ten-minute practice.

As a general rule, you should move your body every twenty-five minutes or so. That way, you're preventing tension from building in your muscle groups. Mother Nature simply did not design our bodies to be sitting down all day. And we must respect her. Speaking of nature . . .

Why It's Time for You to Go "Au Naturel"

How often do you go "au naturel"?
I'm not referring to how often you run around in your birthday suit, even though the well-known French phrase "au naturel" also translates as "nude." (Although if it's something you enjoy, I'd encourage you to do it whenever you can. I know that one of my students does the "Cloudy Hands" Qi Gong routine naked just to get her husband to practice with her. She says it works like magic. Hey, do what works to get your partner to do something fun and healthy.)

I'm talking about how often you get in touch with Mother Nature. "Au naturel," also more directly translated as "the natural state,"[1] is a state of being that we really should tap into more. The body has not caught up with our new modern environments and is certainly not a fan of concrete office blocks, long car journeys, flashing lights, constant noise, and being trapped within four walls for days on end. We're just not built for it. No wonder we get stir-crazy when we've been out of touch with nature, and all her cycles, for too long.

Take light, for example. Biologically, our bodies are unable to tell the difference between the sun and artificial lighting, especially blue light, which is emitted by screens of any kind: your laptop, your TV, your phone, etc. That means that if you're watching a movie in the evening, your brain will suppress the secretion of melatonin (the sleep hormone), often rendering you unable to fall asleep. Quite simply, to your body, you're in broad daylight . . . so why would it be an appropriate time to catch some z's? Back in the day, we spent our evenings in the comforting, relaxing darkness, with the only lights being those of the moon and stars and, later in our history, golden candlelight. Both these conditions were optimal for the body's circadian rhythm. Although the invention of artificial light has served us immensely, our bodies are paying the price.[2]

Our evolution into an age of "convenience" is beginning to take its toll on our waistlines too. Whereas before, we'd have to run after our meat and forage for our morning berries, now everything is available 24/7 with no effort whatsoever. With the online shopping revolution, we now no longer even have to visit the grocery store to fill our fridges. But what happens when you combine a body built for fat storage (because it still thinks you need to prepare for a cold, harsh, hungry winter) with zero exercise and zero boundaries when it comes to food choices? Obesity. No wonder most American adults are overweight or obese. The stats are in: 72.7 percent of us are overweight and run all the health risks that come with it.[3]

Worse, there's the impact of stress on our bodies, which we covered in the "Slow Mind" section. In short, being too immersed in the stress and convenience of modern-day living can slowly kill the primal body. That's where our Pachamama (an Andean word for Mother Earth/Mother Nature) can swoop in and save the day. Our bodies are built to be in nature and automatically relax when they return to the environments they're designed for. Moreover, we can connect with nature as a way to power up the body and refresh our systems with clean energy and a sense of vitality.

Are you ready to go "au naturel" once more for the sake of the temple of your one and only soul?

QUICK MYTH: Nature is somewhere we used to live—but in the twenty-first century, it's old news. We don't need nature anymore.

SLOW REALITY: Being within and around nature is vital for the health of our bodies and minds.

Exercise #8: Slow Down with Nature's Big Five

Not all of us have the pleasure of having direct access to the natural wonders of the world. A much-needed sense of perspective cannot always be obtained at the peak of Mount Everest. The northern lights cannot be launched on demand, and we can't take a dip in the Pacific Ocean to lovingly gaze upon the Great Barrier Reef whenever the whim takes us. The traditional and awe-inspiring "Big Five" (the lion, leopard, rhino, elephant, and African buffalo) aren't animals that tend to approach us in our local green spaces. Because of this, I wanted to share my own Big Five that nature provides to the vast majority of us without the need for extensive travel or effort. These protocols happen to be taught by the best Qi Gong masters out there.

When you go out into nature, there's often a feeling of slowing down and entering the moment. People are naturally drawn to nature. The most expensive real estate often has nature all around; from oceanfronts to mountaintops, we are seeking ways to connect to our source.

Our Qi Gong–endorsed Big Five is as follows:

1. Grass/soil/sand
2. Sun
3. Stars
4. Water
5. Trees

Now, my guess is that you have access to at least one of those things. And each will help you slow down, feel connected, and tune in to nature.

Let's start from the ground up.

Grounding Yourself on Grass, Soil, or Sand

There are various impressive studies on grounding, also known as "earthing," that prove its benefit-rich results on the human body.

Grounding entails the simple practice of taking off your shoes and socks and allowing your bare feet to touch the earth. Modern life demands a consistent covering of the feet in outdoor spaces, and most of us do so to protect the soles of our feet. But it turns out that we could be missing out on a major health-boosting hack. You see, direct physical contact with the huge amount of electrons on the surface of the earth has been recognized as a catalyst for improved human well-being, a sense of peace, connection to nature, and physical healing, including better sleep and reduced pain.[4]

>**Step 1**: Choose your natural ground (grass, soil, and sand are great options), and take off your shoes and socks.
>
>**Step 2**: Maintain direct contact between your bare feet and the natural ground while focusing on the cool or warm sensation and taking calm, deep breaths.
>
>**Step 3**: Stand up straight or gently walk around, feeling your skin on the natural earth for at least 30 seconds, and enjoy all the psychophysical benefits.
>
>**Step 4**: Take some slow, deep breaths. Feel a sense of connection to the earth below. Imagine that you have energetic roots growing through the bottom of your feet into the earth. When you exhale, imagine old, stagnant energy leaving your body. When you inhale, imagine fresh, healing energy coming into your body.

Doing this for even 1 minute can deoxidize the body and replenish the negative ions. In nature, negative ions are much higher than in cities, and studies have shown that increased contact with ions increases the flow of oxygen to the brain, directly influencing your levels of mental energy and alertness.[5]

Enjoy a Sunrise or Sunset

Now, I know this one is weather permitting, as we can never guarantee clear skies. But what we can guarantee is that the sun will rise and set. So whenever you have a day where visibility is good, I recommend getting out to see as many sunrises and sunsets as you can. Because these moments arouse a sense of profound beauty and awe, it's no wonder that #sunrise or #sunset are some of the most popular Instagram hashtags of all time. But it's not just your Instagram feed that will benefit from this cost-free natural show. It's also your body's circadian rhythm, your mood, and even your sociability.[6]

Step 1: Wake up early to enjoy a sunrise, or organize your day so you can watch the sunset. Make sure the environment is as distraction-free as possible.

Step 2: Situate yourself in front of this visual treat at least 10 minutes before the sun rises fully or disappears over the horizon.

Step 3: Watch the entire process mindfully, with as much attention as possible, taking deep breaths and reveling in a sense of wonder and well-being. After all, you get only so many trips around the sun.

Gaze at the Stars

I love the famous quotation by genius Stephen Hawking: "Remember to look up at the stars and not down at your feet. Try to make sense of what you see and wonder about what makes the universe exist. Be curious. And however difficult life may seem, there is always something you can do and succeed at."[7] If it's good enough for Hawking, it's good enough for me. What's more, much like watching the sun rise or set, stargazing has been proven to support your body's sacred circadian rhythm, decrease stress, and even sharpen your eyesight.[8]

Step 1: Check the weather in advance for the best time to stargaze during the evening.

Step 2: Head to a spot where light pollution won't interfere with your experience, be it a park, the beach, or even up a mountain if that's available to you. If you're interested in making a trip out of it, I recommend Googling the best places on Earth to go stargazing—there are a lot of useful blogs and articles to help you choose.

Step 3: Switch off your phone, sit back, and allow yourself to do nothing but stare at the stars for at least 10 minutes. Let your mind be clear, and allow yourself to feel the vast power of the universe and your place within it, knowing that your mind and body will thank you for it.

Get Wet, or at Least Spend Time Around Water

The ocean. The rivers. The lakes. The streams. If there's running water around, I want you to find it! Just being around water is incredible for your body and mind, but add swimming into the mix, and you've got yourself the healthiest cocktail (or mocktail, should I say) you could dream of. Take swimming in the sea, for example. As well as providing a gorgeous setting for some bone- and joint-friendly exercise, the water itself is also swimming in benefits. Rich in magnesium, amino acids, and antibacterial microorganisms, seawater has been proven to cleanse swimmers of stress, relax their muscles, promote deeper sleep, and stimulate the parasympathetic system. This in and of itself can trigger the release of the "happy hormones" dopamine and serotonin.[9] If you don't have a beach nearby, don't worry. The mere act of spending some time around natural sources of water has an incredibly positive effect on the mind and body. (Especially running water, which mimics the sound of "white noise," proven to promote higher cognitive function and increase the body's production of feel-good chemicals.)[10]

Step 1: Whip out a map and see where your local natural water source resides. Maybe it's the ocean or perhaps a lake in a nearby park. As long as it's natural, it counts.

Step 2: Decide whether you will swim in the water or just look from afar. If you plan to swim, be sure to grab swimming attire and a towel and make sure you're allowed to swim there. If you choose to just watch the water, you have several options: you can sit on a bench or on the ground or even go for a mindful walk on the shore—the choice is yours. Observe the ripples and movements, paying attention to the sun's glittering reflection on the water, and feel your worries melt away. (The last time I did this, my shoulders literally fell away from my ears—I had no idea I was even holding any tension there.)

Step 3: If you're swimming, submerge yourself in the water while breathing slowly, feeling the smooth texture of the water on your skin, and swimming for at least 5 minutes. If you're observing a body of water, use your senses of sight and hearing to really pay attention to the way the water moves and flows and the comforting sounds it makes as it does. Sit back, relax, and allow your system to soak up the health benefits.

Get Dry and Forest Bathe

Known as the Japanese practice of Shinrin-yoku, forest bathing is fast becoming one of the most popular biohacks of our time, and for good reason. The simple yet highly effective exercise of heading to your local forest and being among an abundance of trees is proving to be amazing for mental and physical health. Forest bathing has been shown to regulate high blood pressure, reduce the levels of glucose in your blood, balance your endocrine system (which affects your hormones), relieve a plethora of mental disorders, help heal cancer, improve your immunity, and fight respiratory diseases.[11] This method of being tranquil and quiet among the trees and using mindfulness to observe the beauty and wisdom of the nature around you may well be just the ticket to 360 well-being.

Step 1: Head to your local woods or to a green space with plenty of trees. You'll want to spend at least 15 minutes there to get all the benefits, so plan for this in your schedule.

Step 2: As you walk among the trees, make a commitment to slow down and focus solely on observing the roots, trunks, branches, and leaves of the trees that surround you. Feel a sense of peace wash over you, and observe the tension release from your body.

Step 3: For an added bonus, imagine that the trees you're observing are breathing through their bark, and breathe with them. Imagine that your inhales and exhales are synced, you breathing through your nose and the trees through their woody exterior. After all, you are breathing the same air together.

My hope is that you're now feeling much more inspired to move your body, get into flow, and be at one with nature. The benefits aren't just physical but also mental and spiritual. So let's take a step back to our natural selves, into our natural environments, and into a slower, more peaceful way of living.

Going Deeper

Fuel for the Body

Now that we have an understanding of how to move our bodies in an optimal way, as well as where to place them in the world (nature, please), we'll turn our attention to what we put inside them. Before we begin, be aware that calories, weight, and food behavior will be mentioned in this section, so if you're currently struggling with an eating disorder of any kind or perhaps feel that this content could trigger you, please feel free to skip this section. That said, this is a figuratively guilt-free space, and what you're about to learn goes way beyond eating your greens and sugar-shaming. For me, it's the *how* and the *why* of disordered eating that eventually cause our bodies issues. It's not so much *what* you eat that's the main problem, in my opinion, but we'll start there.

We all indulge in comfort food from time to time. The British often turn to tea and biscuits, the Chinese comfort the soul with warm congee or the increasingly popular bubble tea, the Spanish go for churros with chocolate, the French snarf freshly baked croissants in the mornings, and the Italians have their delicious gelato.

Sugar, oh honey, honey, is undeniably delicious. No wonder we're all left wanting more. But it's not just sugary foods that comfort us;

it's food in general, as long as there's enough of it. According to the American Psychological Association, 38 percent of adults claimed to have overeaten or eaten unhealthy foods in the past month. What's more, half of these people also reported irregular eating and overindulgence on a weekly basis.[1]

Having junk food occasionally is unlikely to cause any lasting damage. But bingeing on it on a regular basis after an evening meal of a burger and fries that you have at least three nights a week, washed down with a Budweiser . . . well, that's where it can start to get problematic. And my friend Barbara knew this.

"I don't just eat when I'm hungry," she confessed. "I eat to relax."

When I first met Barbara, she had been on a diet for nineteen years. After almost two decades of yo-yo dieting, her eating habits were a constant issue and had wreaked havoc on both her health and her self-esteem. She had tried everything from low fat to low carb, from keto and paleo to liquid diets. If you have tried any of these diets, you know that although they can be effective in the short term, they're not always sustainable. On a practical level, completely cutting out sugar and carbs in a country like the United States will leave you with a very limited social life. Then there's the emotional level. The fact that nearly a billion people in the world are overweight[2] proves that nutrition often has nothing to do with it.

Why Do We Stuff Our Bodies at the Buffet?

Why do people overeat? Well, there are many viable reasons that the average Joe partakes in overeating.

One of the reasons, as we've covered, is our emotional state. Eating yummy food is a very comforting, pleasurable distraction from the pain we may be feeling inside. The food companies know this all too well. And once the pleasure starts, you don't want it to end, especially with sugar and carbs, due to the way your primal brain is wired. We're still running on the cavepeople "WINTER IS COMING" programming, which is why it's so hard to override the ancestral desire to eat and eat and eat.

Then there's our culture. I'm talking about Christmas, Easter, Thanksgiving, and birthdays, to name a few . . . and they're all heavily centered around eating more than your fair share. What's more, we all want to feel abundant on those occasions and eat, well, abundantly. Overeating has been practiced quite consciously and deliberately from the ancient Romans in ceremonious feasts of plenty (followed by throwing it all up again to make room for more) to the modern American who goes a little overboard at the local diner. Be honest: do you know anyone who would prefer a salad box when everyone else is enjoying themselves at the all-you-can-eat buffet?

Then there's the speed at which we eat. Sometimes we eat so quickly that we don't even know we've gone overboard with our portion sizes. Did you know that it takes roughly twenty minutes after you've swallowed your food for your brain to register that your stomach is full?[1]

Contributing to this is the fact that we now tend to eat in a very distracted way. Lunch at our desk while reading our pending emails and dinner in front of the TV are far-from-uncommon rituals. But eating mindlessly renders us vulnerable to overeating.

In this section, I'll share the slow, secret key to healthy eating. And don't worry; it doesn't involve ditching your treats on a weekend. It's not solely *what* you eat that ends up causing obesity and other health issues. It's *how* you eat.

> **QUICK MYTH:** Eating is just about filling your tank, so ingesting food as quickly as possible, whenever you feel like it, is fine.
>
> **SLOW REALITY:** Eating is about much more than just nutrition; it's about culture, slowing down, and connecting to pleasure. That said, it should never be relied upon as a crutch to avoid emotional pain.

Barbara's Revolution

If I was going to support Barbara on a path toward better health, I knew I had to get to the number-one root cause of her toxic eating patterns. She revealed, in her words, that she "ate to relax." She'd done so ever since her days as a teenager in an abusive household, where her stepfather would routinely wreck the house in fits of rage. She would hide away and eat sweets unconsciously and quickly to make herself feel better. The challenge was that Barbara had created some pretty strong neural connections between "food" and "feel better" over a lot of years, which of course needed to be addressed. But the good news was that eating was not the only way to find tranquility.

Sometimes, I told Barbara, it's true that eating can calm us, reduce stress, and even help us feel more grounded in a chaotic world. But eating isn't the best way to get there. I explained that calming down is a healthy intention and that finding ways to feel good is a noble quest. It's better than just staying down in the dumps, but stress eating isn't the way to go, as she had been caught in a vicious cycle. She, like many others, had adopted an unhealthy behavior (overeating) that didn't match her intention (to feel better).

I told Barbara we could calm her system without using food as a crutch. And I'm happy to say she went for it—and succeeded. More on how she did so later in this chapter.

I helped many people like Barbara through my work with Weight Watchers. Weight Watchers is an international company that helps people forge better eating habits and has a particularly high number of success stories in the United States and the United Kingdom. During my time there, I'm delighted to report that 92 percent of the Weight Watchers members reported feeling better, more motivated, and able to make healthier choices. Although the name of the organization implies that it's all about weight loss, it's actually more about forging a healthy, happy lifestyle. The program I ran using the Slow Principles turned out to be the highest-rated program that the company had ever piloted. It was named "Qi Flow," part of the "Beyond the Scale" program. Our findings were that achieving food freedom and health was about much more than just counting calories. It had to do with a variety of principles like stress management, when and how we consume food, sleep, body movement, and the emotional state of the person while chewing their meals.

Barbara partook in all the exercises and habit changes you're reading about. She is no longer obese, has far more energy than before, and lives life passionately and confidently.

Without further ado, let's dive into the Slow Principles for eating that you can start experimenting with today.

Eat S-L-O-W-L-Y

It's not always *what* you eat but *how* you eat that creates physical wellness.

The *how* affects the *what* too. And we'll start with how quickly, or how slowly, you choose to eat your meals.

One of the most important benefits of eating slowly is that it gives your body time to recognize that you're full. As you now know, it takes about twenty minutes from the start of a meal for the brain to send out satiety signals. But most people's meals don't last that long. Imagine the extra food you're ingesting simply because you didn't allow your body enough time to register that full tummy!

As we've discussed, this conundrum is intrinsically linked to our culture: we are rushed, distracted, and too busy, which has a strong negative effect on the way we eat. Most people in North America eat fast—too fast. No wonder we're the world's biggest producers of "fast food" as well as the biggest fast-food consumers.[1] We eat food that's dripping with fat and sugar, and we wolf it down at the speed of light because we have other priorities than eating. We "overshoot the runway," meaning that we tend to finish meals before our natural satiety signals kick in and therefore end up suddenly—uncomfortably—overstuffed.

At the University of Rhode Island, researchers examined how eating speed affected the amount of food we eat by observing sixty participants consume a meal. Their findings were surprising:

- Slow eaters consumed 2 ounces of food per minute
- Medium-speed eaters consumed 2.5 ounces of food per minute
- Fast eaters consumed 3.1 ounces per minute. They also took larger bites and chewed less before swallowing[2]

This means that fast eaters are not only putting away more food but also consuming more calories and receiving fewer satiety signals than slow eaters.

They conducted a similar study of thirty women of a similar body type who were told to eat a ginormous plate of pasta. The participants were served the same lunch on two different occasions. During each dining experience, the researchers instructed the women to eat to the point of comfortable fullness. However, during the first visit, they were told to eat as quickly as possible, while on the second visit, they were asked to eat slowly. When the researchers compared the difference in food consumption between the quickly eaten lunch and the slowly eaten lunch, they found that the participants consumed fewer calories when they ate slowly.[3]

If you extrapolate that to three meals per day, seven days per week, you can see how quickly those extra calories could add up. Here's another interesting twist: the women reported more hunger an hour after their quickly eaten lunch than they did after their slowly eaten lunch. So eating quickly not only led to greater food consumption but actually satisfied the women less. Conversely, of course, slow eating meant less food but more long-lasting satisfaction and a sense of fullness.

If that's not enough to inspire slowness, check this out. Fast eating and low chewing have also been linked to a 35 percent increase in a person's risk for metabolic syndrome.[4] Metabolic syndrome, for those who aren't familiar with the medical term, is a mix of diabetes, high blood pressure (hypertension), and obesity. Let's just say it's not something you want to add to your medical conditions profile.

Much like the fast eaters in the numerous studies we've looked at, many of us (even though we may not have weight issues) neglect to take the time to savor our food . . . or even to chew it properly. And that's important because, by not chewing your food properly, you're seriously compromising your quality of digestion. "Drink your food, chew your liquid" is a classic Taoist saying, meaning we should chew our food to liquid and swill liquid around in the mouth before swallowing. People have been advising others to chew their food well for a long, long time. In Chinese medicine, slow and thorough chewing is considered essential to strong digestive health, helping to separate a food's indigestible components from its necessary nutrients.

Modern science has confirmed that digestion starts in the mouth. When we chew our food, the enzymes in our saliva start to break it down into something that the body can absorb and assimilate.[5] If you fail to chew properly, you deprive your body of the first stage of digestion. And if step one is missing, all the other stages of digestion suffer. As you quickly swallow large chunks of food straight into the digestive tract, problems such as painful gas production, bloating, constipation, splitting headaches, and fatigue can quickly set in. In addition, not breaking down your food into smaller particles means that your body cannot absorb all the nutrients, including vital vitamins and minerals, so you run the risk of becoming malnourished and having fermented, undigested food lurking in your gut.

If you're in the market for taking care of your gut, you'll be interested to know that by chewing your food properly and increasing your saliva production, you're also safeguarding the health of your bowels. The reason is a polypeptide found in your saliva that kick-starts a process called the epithelial growth factor (EGF), which is responsible for the development, healing, and general repair of your gut's epithelial tissue.[6]

So there you have it. Lots of reasons to chew your next meal properly—and slowly.

This brings me to the first eating exercise.

(If you have a history of eating disorders, suspect that you may have an eating disorder, or have a family history of eating disorders, these tips may not be for you. Always carry out these eating methods in conjunction with a therapist if this is applicable to you.)

Exercise #9: The 32-Second Chew Rule

According to Intestinal Labs and the most recent science, the optimal number of chews is 32 over a 32-second period.[7] That's 32 chews per mouthful of food.

Obviously, if your dinner tonight is soup, your chewing rate will be a lot lower, and if you're eating a pile of hazelnuts (no judgment here; maybe you're really into hazelnuts), your chewing rate will be higher. But as a general rule, you want to aim for around 30 chews. You really can't chew too much. Remember, your stomach does not have teeth, so it'll take any help it can get.

Here's the challenge: for your next meal, be it breakfast, lunch, or dinner, I want you to chew your food properly. Turn that food to liquid, Taoist style. Chew it 32 times, a little more or a little less depending on the softness of what you're nomming. Your digestive system will thank you for it, and you may find that you eat less than you usually do as you've given your system stronger signals that you're eating, and your brain will have more time to send signals of fullness.

Thirty-two chews per bite, although optimal, is admittedly quite hard to do if you're on a date and are supposed to be listening intently to what the other person is saying. And you can bet your bottom dollar that if you try to count and listen at the same time, you'll sport a vague look in your eyes that's anything but charming and attractive. So if you find yourself in a situation where your attention is split, try to follow the 32-Second Chew Rule for just your first bite. It sets up a pattern for slowing down while eating the rest of the meal.

Taking some extra time to chew your food—especially if you're the type who always finishes dinner first—appears to be a good idea, so please give it a go. After all, we eat for taste and for energy. By chewing your food slowly, you accomplish both of these. When you slow down, you really taste the delicious quality of whatever it is you're eating too. Now, on the subject of deliciousness . . .

Pleasure Through Food

I believe the following to be true: "If more of us valued food and cheer and song above hoarded gold, it would be a merrier world."[1]

Admittedly, that's not my quotation. Any Lord of the Rings fans will recognize it from J. R. R. Tolkien's *The Hobbit*. Whether uttered in a fictional tavern in the mountains of Middle Earth or your local Whole Foods, the sentiment remains the same.

So much value and pleasure can be found in eating. Yes, we eat to nourish ourselves and fuel our bodies, but we also should eat to revel in the ecstasy of doing so. The delicious crunch of a fresh green apple, the softness of sourdough toast with creamy butter, the comforting warmth of spices marinating a rainbow of vegetables, the sweet harmony of chocolate melted over dark cherries, and the healing saltiness of chicken soup . . . there's just nothing like the pleasure of eating. It's the only way to stimulate ALL of your senses at the same time.

I see it as a crime when we deny ourselves that level of pleasure.

Eating slowly also helps us feel more satisfied—which is different from just being "full." When you slow down, savor a meal, pay attention to tastes and textures, and appreciate each bite, you leave the table feeling good in your body and mind. Moreover, it will feel like the meal has lasted longer and that you've eaten more, which could prevent and rectify habits of overeating.

When you eat mindfully, you not only give yourself time for unbridled joy but also support your digestive system. You see, when you slow down and take pleasure in your food, your body switches off the fight-or-flight system, aiding optimal digestion. Through "relaxed eating," you can take the wheel and fine-tune the autonomic nervous system to "rest and digest," as it should while you're eating. This way, you also avoid the adverse effects of stress, including the imbalance of the gut's bacteria and the development of irritable bowel syndrome (IBS).[2]

> QUICK MYTH: Nowadays, we have more important responsibilities than eating, so it should be done as swiftly as possible around our busy schedules.
>
> SLOW REALITY: Eating slowly and mindfully is not only important for our health but a precious pleasure to be enjoyed.

Exercise #10: Mealtime Mindfulness

1. Sit down at the table with your meal (yes, a table, not in front of the TV!).
2. Take a second to gaze lovingly at your food.
3. Take a sniff . . . what aromas can you smell?
4. Take a deep breath before taking your first bite.
5. Notice the flavors, textures, and temperature of your food, chewing thoroughly (32 times, remember?) but enjoying the experience. Is it delicious? Allow yourself to let out an "Mmmmm."
6. Put down your knife and fork (or spoon or chopsticks, whatever you're using), and don't be tempted to prepare your next mouthful while eating. Always put down your cutlery between bites.
7. Swallow.

8. Take another deep breath.
9. Pick up your cutlery again and repeat until you feel full.

As you can see, mindfully eating involves using all your senses, slowing down the process, and focusing on one mouthful at a time. Allow yourself this pleasure, and see how you feel afterward.

Combating Fast-Eating Habits with Acupressure

Wendy was in the habit of eating dinner and then sweet treats quickly and mindlessly while watching TV. She did this every night before bed, claiming that it helped her feel less lonely and sad. She used the television screen combined with a large portion of food to generate a feeling of comfort. This is known as "zombie eating." And she's not alone. Up to 91 percent of Americans claim to do the same when eating meals and snacks.[1]

It's no wonder we do this. While walking on the razor-thin line between alertness and anxiety during our working week, we'll take whatever home comforts we can get. We arrive at our final destination, the sofa, wired, tired, and hungry for fulfillment. This is understandable yet problematic because, as we've already established, approaching our eating window with our fight-or-flight system turned on tends to lead to unhealthy eating habits and poor digestion.

As well as practicing the 32-Second Chew Rule and general mindfulness, we can support a healthy dining experience with some much-needed self-care in the form of acupressure. Acupressure has its origins in acupuncture, which was born in ancient China. They're both based on the theory that by stimulating the body's meridians (energy pathways), we can clear stagnation, revitalize our systems, and even prevent numerous diseases.[2] For this chapter, we'll focus on two acupressure point sequences for calming the nervous system, soothing the digestive system, and reducing any intense waves of cravings for unhealthy food that we may experience.

These are simple exercises that can be carried out just before eating a meal or when cravings strike. When stimulated via acupressure, the meridian points I'm about to introduce you to have even been shown to support all kinds of addiction recovery, including alcoholism.[3] I showed Wendy this sequence to first break the connection between TV and food, instructing her to do this *before* turning on the TV and also while watching the TV. It's incredible for those reducing cravings for less-than-nutritious food. Wendy substituted one behavior, eating, for another, self-acupressure. She couldn't believe how simple it was and how it worked so quickly.

Then we introduced a second set of acupressure exercises to enhance her digestion after a meal that was no longer consumed in front of the TV. Wendy, along with many other people I've worked with over the years, claimed that acupressure helped her shut off stress before eating. I urge you to give these exercises a try. You can do them right now as you're reading this book; no special context is necessary.

Exercise #11: Ear Acupressure to Cut Cravings

Auricular acupuncture and acupressure have been proven to help cut even the strongest of cravings.[4] Chinese medicine explains that these miraculous and rapid effects are due to the ear meridian's direct connection with the nervous system. Contrary to popular belief, you do not need needles or special training to reap the benefits. That's the beauty of acupressure, where you massage or tap the meridians as opposed to piercing them with needles.

1. Place your thumbs on the very top part of the front of the ears with your other four fingers behind the ear.
2. Massage the top of the ear in slow, small circles with medium pressure.

3. Take deep breaths as you do so.
4. Keep massaging all the way down the ear to the lobe, the tragus (the bump in front of your ear canal), and the ear canal, continuing the small circles.
5. Massage your way back up to the top of the ears.
6. Repeat this process for 30 seconds to 1 minute to feel the calming effects.

Exercise #12: Acupressure for Optimal Digestion

The pressure point you're about to discover is a very special one. It not only is incredible for optimal digestion and preventing sickness but is also believed to be the key to unlocking secret inner reserves of strength and endurance. As they traversed the expansive countryside to defend their country, Chinese warriors of old adorned themselves with leather sashes sporting stones dangling from either side of their waist. When fatigue set in and their bodies could no longer endure a strenuous hike, the soldiers would take a knee to rest. Serendipitously, the stones would come to rest on the acupressure point known as Stomach 36 on each leg. Upon rising from this position after exerting pressure on the Stomach 36 point, the warriors found themselves infused with renewed strength, enabling them to trek an additional three miles with ease. For this reason, Stomach 36 is also known in acupuncture and acupressure as "Leg Three Mile."

1. Locate the Stomach 36 point four finger widths down from the bottom of your kneecap, along the outer boundary of your shin bone. You can choose to carry out this exercise on whichever leg feels most comfortable, and there is no need to do it on both. If you are in the right place, you should be able to feel a little muscle pop out and in again if you move your foot up and down.

2. Once you've located the point, you can massage the area in small circles or tap it with all your fingers gathered together for optimal precision.
3. Massage or tap with pressure for 30 seconds to 1 minute to support your digestive system (and perhaps even to unlock a secret well of strength within yourself).

A Note on Binge Eating

People who suffer from compulsive eating often feel out of control of their eating behaviors. If not recognized and addressed accordingly, this compulsion to overeat can turn into binge eating disorder. If you've ever experienced a binge episode, you know the feeling—a powerful urge to get the food into your mouth as quickly as possible, consuming a large amount over a short period until you feel uncomfortably full. After a binge, it's common to feel guilty, depressed, ashamed, and regretful.

The good news is that you can often derail a binge or overeating episode—and help yourself get back in the driver's seat—*simply by slowing down*.

In fact, this is a first-aid technique that we used in our Beyond the Scale coaching program for Weight Watchers: when you find yourself in the eye of a binge storm, feeling overwhelmed and at the mercy of an episode, just try to slow down as soon as you realize what's happening. You might not feel able to stop eating right away, and that's okay. But most people *can* slow themselves down a little, even when the binge demons are howling. It's sort of like having someone call your name when you're lost in thought and snap you out of your daydream. This simple "binge slowly" strategy can often shift your attention and help you refocus and regain a sense of food freedom.

Additional Tips for Those Drawn to Binge Eating

1. Use smaller plates for portion control. Use different utensils (chopsticks rather than fork or spoon, or even just smaller forks and spoons).
2. Find another slow eater and pace yourself with them. Picky children and chatty dinner companions who hardly stop blabbering on long enough to take a bite are often ideal for this.
3. Set aside a specific time to eat—at least 20–30 minutes for each meal, and preferably even longer for dinner. You can set a stopwatch on your phone to ensure that you spend enough time eating. Don't just eat "whenever you get around to it" or treat it as an inconvenience. You're fueling your amazing body and maybe spending quality time with friends and family. That's important. It deserves time.

Slow Eating Is the New Black

Most of us lead hectic, fast-paced lives, so it's understandable that we might try to rush our meals. But as we've seen, eating quickly does us no favors.

The research on eating quickly is nearly unanimous: eating quickly makes you feel out of control of your eating habits. Eating slowly will also help you with portion control, stronger feelings of satiety, better mental health, and improved digestion. In contrast, eating quickly leads to poor digestion, increased risk of health issues, and lower satisfaction. The bottom line is this: slow down your eating and enjoy improved health and well-being. Your mind, and of course your body, will thank you for it.

Now that you've learned all about slow movement and slow eating, you've come to the final section of the Slow Body Principle. Take a deep breath.

The Breath as Medicine

Taking Your Vitamin O

A few years back, I began a partnership with a holistic medical doctor in Santa Cruz, California. The idea was to have a place where people could come for treatments from both an Eastern medicine perspective and a holistic Western medicine perspective. We treated patients with acupuncture, herbs, supplements, lifestyle suggestions, movement therapy, and medication when needed.

Tom was a patient whom the doctor and I were treating. He had anxiety, depression, high blood pressure, and digestive issues. He was a high-powered executive, had a wife and two children, and enjoyed backcountry mountaineering. Tom came to us mainly for his anxiety and depression. He was confused about why he felt depressed because he had money, a beautiful family, and a job where he was well respected.

When I sat him down in my treatment room, the first thing Tom told me was "The doc told me I need to learn to breathe. You'd think I'd be better at it; I've been doing it my whole life!"

I laughed with Tom and told him that he wasn't alone. I told him that this doctor was also fond of saying, "If you could put the benefits of deep, slow breathing into a pharmaceutical pill, it would be the best-selling drug in America!" This makes sense from a Chinese medicine perspective. The breath is life, and if we are breathing better, we are living better.

A decade or so ago, my doctor would have been labeled a lunatic to claim that the simple act of breathing properly could heal a person. Until very recently, breathwork may well have been considered a waste of time, practiced only by prayer-bead-wearing hippies. This, however, couldn't be further from the truth. Although I know many a liberal (usually Californian) wellness junkie who's partial to breathwork, it's far from a waste of time, and straitlaced scientists agree.

At the end of the day, the breath keeps us alive, and its absence indicates death. In the Slow lifestyle, our breathing is the quiet, precious foundation. When you breathe properly, you bring balance and vitality to your present-moment experience. There is nothing more important. Think of it this way: how long can you go on living without food? It depends on a few factors, but in general, even the healthiest, fittest human being lasts a couple of weeks. How long can you go without water? Well, that time frame is reduced drastically to just a few days. How long can you survive without breathing? MINUTES.[1]

Yes, my friends, there is no vitamin more vital than your Vitamin O (oxygen).

Having said all this, it stands to reason that we should pay more attention to it. Because even if you're breathing, you can still cause a lot of damage to your body if you're not doing it correctly.

On average, the human being takes twenty-two thousand breaths per day,[2] but not all breaths are made equal. They can bring you stress and panic and cause a depletion of O_2, or they can bring you peace of mind, resilience, and a general feeling of vitality and bliss. The research has now confirmed what Chinese medicine has known for millennia: the way in which you breathe dramatically influences your mental and physical health.[3] Breathwork brings about powerful psychophysiological changes in brain-body interaction, directly influencing the autonomic and central nervous systems. The simple act of conscious breathing may hold the key to near-instant emotional healing and well-being for anyone willing to try it.

For your mental health, breathwork has been proven to

- Decrease symptoms of stress, anger, anxiety, and depression: slow, deep breathing activates the parasympathetic nervous system, which directly calms the body's stress response[4]
- Increase relaxation, inner peace, and joy[5]
- Enhance focus and concentration: slow breathing can help to clear the mind and enhance focus and cognitive abilities[6]
- Deepen self-connection through this simple act of self-care

For your physical health, breathwork has also been proven to

- Improve oxygenation: when we breathe slowly and deeply, we release oxygen stored in the hemoglobin in our blood, which helps to improve our overall oxygenation levels, combating symptoms of fatigue and increasing our overall energy[7]
- Lower blood pressure: slow breathing can dramatically lower high blood pressure, which can reduce the risk of heart disease and stroke[8]
- Help heal asthma naturally: when we breathe optimally, we are able to open once constricted/congested airways and reduce dependency on prescription drugs[9]
- Reduce pain: deep, slow breathing has a direct effect on our perception of pain[10]
- Improve sleep: slow breathing can be helpful in promoting relaxation and better sleep, especially when practiced before bed[11]

It was partially thanks, I believe, to a good friend of mine and an all-around phenomenal human being that breathwork now has a seat at the mainstream health-care table. It was James Nestor who bit the bullet and wrote the best-selling book *Breath: The New Science of a Lost Art*, which brought breathwork into the public eye. In it, he shares how our ability to breathe can have huge effects on our health and well-being in ways we never would have thought possible. James's groundbreaking book proves that deep breathing goes far beyond the confines of inner peace (if that's on the menu, why not take it?), from configuring our facial structures to expanding our airways and assisting us to battle everything from asthma to lung cancer.[12]

How Should You Be Breathing Right Now?

As you read these words, notice your breathing. Without trying to change it, how are you inhaling and exhaling?

Are you breathing in through your nose or mouth? Are you breathing out through the same orifice? Can you feel the breath mostly in your chest, your belly, or a bit of both? How many seconds do the inhales and exhales tend to last?

It's curious because observing the natural breath is much like trying to capture a butterfly: the moment you try to catch it, it flies off in another direction. You need to be quite relaxed and unattached to observe it properly. And once your breath knows you're observing it, it tends to change its behavior. So let go of the judgment and just observe it as subtly and as neutrally as you can. Grab your diary or go to the Notes app on your phone and write down what you've observed about your natural breath. Also write down how you felt while breathing: a bit nervous? Confused? Tense? Happy? Calm?

One of the main things James is asked on a regular basis is "What's the best way to breathe?" The answer is, you guessed it, S-L-O-W. The answer is also multifaceted and depends on the context. If you're just sitting on your behind working or watching TV—in other words, resting and living your life—the answer may be . . . slower than you think. In *Breath*, James shares that the number to remember is 5.5: 5.5-second inhales, 5.5-second exhales, 5.5 breaths per minute. Odds are it's slower than you observed your natural breath to be. But this has been proven to be optimal.

When you breathe slowly, your nervous system relaxes, as we explored earlier. Breathing quickly signals the nervous system that there is imminent danger, and we dive into the fight-or-flight response, which is what we call "stress." We feel tight, tense, and overwhelmed. Slowing down the breath is critical to optimal healing and emotional well-being. At first, you may feel as if you need to breathe more to get the oxygen you feel you need. But James contends that most of us are overbreathers, taking in more oxygen than our bodies actually require to function optimally. What a relatively healthy person should do instead is inhale less for the greatest efficiency, which may seem counterintuitive for oxygenation. But as long as you're breathing slowly and deeply into your belly, your body will do a perfectly fine job of oxygenating itself. Gulping air, in fact, puts pressure on all our systems—for example, it dramatically increases the heart rate, whereas exhaling slowly decreases it. Like overeating, overbreathing is hard on the whole body. When you breathe slowly for 5.5 seconds in and 5.5 seconds out, you become oxygen efficient. Your body has plenty of oxygen stored in the blood. By breathing slowly, it assimilates altitude. With less (but optimal) oxygen coming in, the body reacts by releasing stored oxygen from the hemoglobin and making it available to the cells.

> **QUICK MYTH:** We need oxygen to live, so the more you breathe and the faster you take in oxygen, the better.
>
> **SLOW REALITY:** Slow, controlled breathing leads to optimal oxygenation and a host of health benefits.

Exercise #13: The 5.5 Breathing Rule

Ready to try out the 5.5 breathing protocol? You can practice as you read along. Just pause to count, and repeat.

1. Put one hand on your belly and the other on your chest. Inhale for 5.5 seconds through your nose. (This is a guideline. If 4 seconds feels more comfortable to you at this stage, do that.) As you breathe, you should feel the belly rise first; then your ribcage should expand outward; and then your chest can rise if your lungs are nicely full.
2. Exhale for 5.5 seconds through the nose. (This too is a guideline. If 4 seconds feels more comfortable to you, do that.) Exhaling slowly, let the breath move from the chest down through the ribs and then all the way out of the belly.
3. Repeat 10 to 20 times, breathing rhythmically and slowly.
4. Try to maintain this slow, rhythmic breathing as much as you can while you work and go about your day.

How did this feel?

I'm willing to bet you're a bit more Zen than before. It isn't magic, but I can't think of many well-being practices that come closer to it than breathwork. This simple 5.5 slow breathing technique can be used to reset your system at any point during the day, enabling you to clear stress and shift into a state of mental clarity in a matter of minutes.

BONUS BREATHING ROUTINE: You can stream or download a free video version of this exercise if you go to qigo.ng/slow and select "Exercise #13."

Breathing and Your Emotional Landscape

Breathing is a powerful tool that directly reflects how you feel. Just think about the difference between how you breathe when you're tense and stressed versus when you're riding your bike, working out, making love, or eating a delicious dessert that fills you with pleasure. Compare the breath while you're laughing and crying or just moping around with your head down. What about when you're angry? Have you noticed that the inhale tends to be more challenging than the exhale? It's almost as if we're resisting letting something (or someone) into our space. . . . It's a fascinating concept.

Shortness of breath is often associated with painful, negative emotions, while slow, deep, and smooth breathing usually correlates with pleasant emotions. More interesting still, respiratory patterns aren't influenced only by whatever emotion you happen to be feeling; rather, the way you breathe also directly influences the emotion you feel.[1] It's a bidirectional relationship between the breath and your emotional landscape. They dictate each other in equal measure.

So when you feel happy, you see evidence of this in your triumphant inhales and relaxed long exhales. When you feel sad, you see evidence of this in your shallow inhales and labored exhales. If you want to feel happy instead? *Breathe like it until you feel it.*

The breath allows us to hit the reset button on our emotions. With breath training, we become emotional master chefs, cooking up whatever emotions serve us at any given time. It's incredible how something as simple as changing our breathing can bring about what's most important to us. When we break it down, we all want to feel peace and happiness. And there's a breath for that.

Exercise #14: Vagal Breathing: The Breath of Joy

This technique has been used for centuries in various Eastern cultures and traditions, including Yoga, meditation, and martial arts, which refer to it as "the cleansing breath." In the West, we call it "Vagal Breathing." Vagal Breathing, also known as abdominal breathing, is a breathing technique that involves consciously inhaling, pausing, exhaling, and pausing again, all the while using your diaphragm muscle (the one in your lower belly).

The vagus nerve is a long nerve that runs all the way from your brain stem down through the neck and into the chest and abdomen. It plays a critical role in regulating the body's autonomic nervous system (which, if you remember, controls involuntary bodily functions such as your heart rate, digestion, and, when you're not thinking about it, breathing). When you practice Vagal Breathing, you activate this special vagus nerve, which in turn stimulates the parasympathetic nervous system. This is the system mentioned earlier that's responsible for rest and relaxation, counteracting the body's fight-or-flight stress response.

Vagal Breathing can be done in a variety of ways, but this one is my favorite. I call it "The Breath of Joy," and it can be used whenever you feel the need for an extra boost of peace and happiness.

1. Find a comfortable position sitting or lying down.
2. Place a hand on your belly so you can direct the breath there.
3. Breathe in for the count of 4, feeling your diaphragm move your belly outward.
4. Hold your breath for 2 seconds.
5. Breathe out for the count of 8, feeling your belly deflate and relax back in.

6. Hold your breath again for just a short moment, a split second, before inhaling again.

Repeat this process for several minutes, focusing on your breath and allowing yourself to relax. If you feel dizzy, please try it again with shorter in-breaths and out-breaths: rather than the 4-2-8 seconds, try 4-2-4, inhaling for 4 seconds, holding for 2 seconds, and exhaling for 4 seconds. This technique can be done at any time, but it's particularly useful when you're feeling stressed or anxious to calm down your entire system. Many people choose to breathe this way before sleeping to wipe the energetic slate clean and fall asleep in a calmer, more contented fashion.

When we optimize our breathing in this way and create the correct internal and energetic balance, miraculous physiological changes occur through increased oxygenation, breathing coordination, and nervous system balance. This affects the entire human organism and its billions of functions, including all of the subtle energy systems such as meridians (the body's energetic pathways).

And we're just scratching the surface. The sheer power of breathing still remains mysterious. But James Nestor, I, and our global community of "Pulmonauts," as James affectionately calls us, can testify to the benefits. James is leading a revolution in breathwork. But it wouldn't be a complete chapter on the power of breathing if I didn't mention the other, now celebrity-status Pulmonaut who goes by the title of "the Iceman." And he's taken the power of breathwork to the extreme.

BONUS BREATHING ROUTINE: You can stream or download a free video version of this exercise if you go to qigo.ng/slow and select "Exercise #14."

Breaking the Ice with Wim Hof

Wim Hof, aka "the Iceman," is a Dutch superhero who has set multiple world records for his feats of endurance. But instead of a cape, he wears nothing but shorts in the snow. He's known for his hugely impressive stunts, such as running a half-marathon barefoot above the Arctic Circle, suppressing his immune response (seriously, he had endotoxins injected into his bloodstream and didn't break a sweat[1]), and staying quite comfortably in a container filled with ice cubes for over two hours. How? By *breathing*.

The Wim Hof Method, which involves breathing exercises, meditation, and cold exposure, has taken the world by storm. Scientists are studying Wim to this day, and he has no intention of impeding their research on what is humanly possible.

In 2018, someone who was interviewing me asked jovially, "If you could have a lunch date with anyone alive on the planet, who would it be?" I thought long and hard, and it was a toss-up between Oprah and Wim Hof. It was a tough choice. I eventually told my interviewer that because Wim Hof was (quite literally) the coolest human being around, he'd be my final choice.

A little over a year later, in 2019, my wildest lunch-date dream actually came true. I got to sit down with Wim Hof, the revered Iceman himself, and pick his brain about all things breathwork and immunity. He just happened to be in San José, California, for an all-day conference and Wim Hof Method workshop. Wim welcomed me with open arms, and before we could even hit "record" on the camera, he dove into the ins and outs of the magic to be found in breathwork. He literally couldn't contain his enthusiasm as he shared his personal experiences with me. His passion was infectious. Wim told me all about the crazy lab experiments he had been a part of recently and how he had been injected with the Ebola virus in one study to test the effects of his breathing techniques on his immune system. The craziest part? Wim felt no symptoms, discomfort, or illness after the injection. I was blown away—this guy truly had a superhuman immune system.

In his smooth, Dutch accent, he said it was all about the breath. I didn't even have to ask him any questions. Wim was doing all the talking, and I wasn't about to stop him. He broke down complex research on his immune system and some additional science behind cold exposure. Before we knew it, an hour had gone by and it was time for Wim to run his workshop onstage in front of thousands of people.

And before *I* knew it, Wim was dragging me onstage to take his attendees through a Qi Gong sequence to tap into relaxation and a sense of centeredness before diving into the breathwork. It was a truly incredible afternoon.

According to Wim, we should breathe in deep, rhythmic patterns into the belly on a regular basis. A lot of us breathe into the chest nowadays due to stress, so to fully oxygenate the body, you want to be using your diaphragm. In a typical breathwork session, Wim would take you through thirty deep breaths, inhaling through the nose (or even mouth if you want a very intense experience) and exhaling through the mouth, followed by holding the breath for as long as possible. This cycle should be repeated for several rounds, and it's important to be in a relaxed state during it. Thousands of people have been trained in this method by Wim Hof himself and practice this breathing technique daily to help reduce stress and anxiety.

Wim's breathing techniques are based on Tibetan Tummo breathing, which I'll teach you how to practice safely in the next section. "Tummo" is a Tibetan word that translates to "inner fire"; this breathing technique can increase your ability to tolerate extremely cold temperatures and improve overall health and well-being. Tummo breathing is used by Tibetan Buddhist monks to warm themselves in the coldest, most bitter winters when temperatures drop to −2.2° Fahrenheit. Along with a self-generated inner heat, this sort of breathing is believed to increase our ability to control our physiological responses (just as Wim does in the labs).

I argue that the kind of breathing that Wim primarily does is not for beginners. So for the sake of this book, I have curated a deep oxygenation sequence for you to try that will enable you to reap many of the same benefits in a similar way. Its roots derive directly from Tummo breathing, and I call it Go Fast to Go Slow Breathing. The pace is quite fast, which you may think contrasts with the title of this book. *I thought I was trying to slow my breathing* DOWN? you may well be thinking. But advanced slow practices often play with polarity. It's like when you want to get stronger at the gym. First, you have to induce weakness in the muscles by tearing the muscle fibers in the name of building stronger muscles down the road. And just like strength training, the following practice should be carried out only in short bursts to build up your lung capacity and optimization.

Ready to give it a go?

Exercise #15: Go Fast to Go Slow Breathing

Find a comfortable and quiet place where you can sit or lie down without being disturbed. If you tend to get dizzy easily, please do this lying down.

1. Take a few slow, deep breaths to calm your mind and relax your body.
2. Begin taking around 30 deep breaths in quick succession. Breathe in deeply through your nose, and exhale through your mouth. Each breath should be deep enough to fill your lungs completely. Note that the inhale and the exhale shouldn't take longer than 1 second each.

3. Picture the breaths you're taking fanning an imaginary fire in your abdomen.
4. After you've completed the deep breaths, exhale fully and hold your breath for just 5 to 10 seconds.
5. As you take in your next inhalation, do so as slowly as you possibly can. Because you've oxygenated your body to the max, you'll be able to breathe a lot slower than you usually would. If you're interested in keeping track of such details, count how slowly you can breathe in and how slowly you can breathe out, and write it down.
6. Practice 5.5-second breathing again and witness how effortless it is.
7. Notice how you feel. Most people who practice Go Fast to Go Slow Breathing report feeling a profound sense of inner peace and slowness.

Tips for practicing Go Fast to Go Slow Breathing:

- Always practice this breathwork in a safe and controlled environment, and never when you're driving or operating heavy machinery. (I know you wouldn't, but I have to say it!)
- If you feel lightheaded or dizzy, stop the practice and take a break.
- Listen to your body and don't force it to do anything too uncomfortable.
- You can gradually increase the number of breaths and hold time as you become more comfortable with the technique.

BONUS BREATHING ROUTINE: You can stream or download a free video version of this exercise if you go to qigo.ng/slow and select "Exercise #15."

Why You Need to Shut Your Mouth

Did you know that there's a saying in Eastern medicine that goes "The mouth is for eating, the nose is for breathing"? Although that's a straightforward concept, you'd be surprised at how many of us use our mouths instead of our noses to suck in air. And if that sounds like an unimportant detail, you're mistaken.

You'll notice that the technique I shared above was based on just *exhaling* through the mouth, not breathing *in* through it. Even an extreme breath enthusiast like Wim wouldn't suggest mouth breathing as a safe lifestyle option. I'm acknowledging here that although the Iceman often chooses to carry out his breathwork training through the mouth, he does so because it's for extremely short periods. You can rest assured that he does not inhale through his mouth in general. The only time you should be breathing through your mouth is for an EXHALE, and only if you're practicing breathwork, bursting out in fits of laughter, or doing hard-core exercise. All our fellow mammals would agree with this decision. We all have nostrils and mouths to breathe out of, but the first choice for any four-legged friend is always the nose.

Why?

Breathing primarily through your mouth can lead to a number of potential dangers and health issues. Here are a few to breathe into:

- Reduced oxygen intake: when you breathe through your mouth, you're not able to take in as much oxygen as you would when breathing through your nose. This can lead to fatigue, brain fog, snoring, and sleep apnea.[1]

- Dry mouth: breathing through your mouth can cause dryness in your mouth and throat, leading to bad breath, tooth decay, and gum disease.[2]
- Increased risk of infection: the nose has tiny hairs called cilia that help to filter harmful particles and bacteria out of the air you breathe. Breathing through your mouth bypasses this natural filter, increasing your risk of infection and chronic illness in your throat, lungs, and other parts of your body. (This one has been common knowledge since the 1800s.)[3]
- Dental problems: mouth breathing can lead to misaligned teeth, an overbite, and even changes to the shape of your face over time.[4]
- Impaired speech development: children and adults who breathe primarily through their mouths may have difficulty developing proper speech and suffer speech deficits.[5]

Concerning, right? Overall, it's important to breathe through your nose as much as possible to avoid these potential dangers and promote good health. Simple.

You see, the nose is one of the body's most overlooked powerhouses. It's our body's primary defense against all sorts of nasty germs, impurities, dust, and bacteria that could sneak into our lungs, bloodstream, and other parts of our body. The nose has bacilli-fighting glands, mucous membrane passages, and thousands of filtering hairs to protect us from harm and stop any lurking bad guys from waltzing right in.

Breathing through the nose also allows all that fresh air to penetrate the body more deeply, expanding all the way down to our lower abdomen. And let's not forget about the diaphragm—the unsung hero of healthy breathing. When we breathe through the nose, we naturally use the diaphragm, just as babies and children do.

So whatever you do, breathe through your nose for the most part, not your mouth. There are specific techniques that use mouth breathing to help us achieve certain goals, but 98 percent of the time, breathe through the nose if possible. This is something you can consciously control. If you're currently a mouth breather and need some extra support, try setting hourly alarms on your phone to remind you to breathe through your nose. What if you breathe through your mouth as you sleep? you ask. Try taping your mouth. Seriously—go to your local pharmacist or buy it online. It's inexpensive, and although you may need to trade your sex appeal for the training, it'll be totally worth it in the long run. (And you won't snore anymore, so you'll get extra brownie points from whomever you're sharing your bed with.)

> **QUICK MYTH:** Mouth breathing gets oxygen into the body faster than nose breathing, and there's nothing wrong with it. That's why you gasp for air through your mouth!
>
> **SLOW REALITY:** Mouth breathing is not only suboptimal for oxygenation but can also lead to health issues such as sleep apnea, dental problems, and increased risk of infection. Slow nasal breathing is vital to your well-being.

Exercise #16: Getting Friendly with Your Nasal Passages

If you're new to nasal breathing or want to improve the quality of your breathing and open those sinuses, getting to know your nostrils with alternate-nostril breathing is a great way to start.

Alternate-nostril breathing, also known as Nadi Shodhana or Anulom Vilom Pranayama, is an ancient yogic breathing technique that involves alternating the flow of breath through the left and right nostrils. It is a powerful dynamic meditation that can also help calm the mind and dramatically reduce stress and anxiety, which can consequently lower the breather's blood pressure and promote better sleep.[6]

Ready to get started? Set aside five minutes and carry out the following steps:

1. Find a comfortable seated position with your spine straight and your shoulders relaxed.
2. Place your left hand on your left knee, palm facing up.
3. Bring your right hand up to your face and use your index and middle fingers to close your left nostril.
4. Inhale deeply through your right nostril, filling your lungs with air.
5. Pause briefly at the top of your inhale.
6. Use your thumb to close your right nostril, and exhale through your left nostril.
7. Pause briefly at the bottom of your exhale.
8. Inhale deeply through your left nostril.
9. Pause briefly at the top of your inhale.
10. Use your index and middle fingers to close your left nostril, and exhale through your right nostril.
11. Pause briefly at the bottom of your exhale.
12. Repeat steps 4–11 for several rounds, focusing on your breath and maintaining a slow and steady pace.

How do you feel?

Alternate-nostril breathing can be practiced for a few minutes at a time or for longer periods, depending on your needs and preferences. It is best to start with a few minutes and gradually increase the duration as you become more comfortable with the alternative way to breathe.

BONUS BREATHING ROUTINE: You can stream or download a free video version of this exercise if you go to qigo.ng/slow and select "Exercise #16."

Breathe, Just Breathe

This life can be hard. And when the going gets tough, it becomes tough to breathe. But you must. It's the only key to finding peace again in your mind and your body.

In the heart-wrenching scene when protagonist Neo discovers the sad and shocking truth about unconscious human existence in the 1999 science fiction action movie *The Matrix*, he begins to show signs of a mental breakdown. He has just learned that the world he thought was real is actually an elaborate illusion. He's shaky on his feet, aggressive to those surrounding him, and in denial, and he struggles to focus his eyes. Morpheus, an ever-wise and efficient leader in the revolt against the oppressive Matrix, offers Neo one piece of advice: "Breathe, Neo. Just. Breathe."

The breath is life, but it is also a direct reflection of your quality of life. To breathe deeper is to delve more fully into the human experience, and the proper functioning of every single cell in your body depends upon the quality of the way you go about it. Breathing unites all living things in an invisible yet necessary symbiotic life-support system.

The Earth needs it. You need it. And whether you need to calm yourself in a crisis, focus on your mission, help your body to heal, or lay it down to rest, your breath is always here for you.

It's the first thing you ever did. It's the last thing you'll ever do. So let's start treating breathwork as the quiet miracle, and utmost priority, that it is.

To the Heart of the Matter

Now that you've learned all about how to bring slowness to your physical body, it's time to slow down your heart.

I can hear you now . . .

"Wait a minute, Lee, I think you'll find the heart is part of the body, and I sure as hell don't want that to slow down too much."

The heart I'm referring to is figurative; it's your center of emotions, love, and compassion that transcends its role as a blood pumper. And it's good that it does because we have the figurative heart to thank for the quality of our personal relationships. Our healthy, loving connection to others is a vital ingredient of a happy life and, consequently, the third Slow Principle.

Principle 3

SLOW RELATIONSHIPS

A loving heart [is] better and stronger than wisdom.

—Charles Dickens

You've got the heart of a lion. Cross your heart. Eat your heart out. Don't take it to heart. Put your heart into it. Pour your heart out. Follow your heart. Your heart is in the right place.

There's a reason the English language showcases the heart in so many idioms. It goes without saying that our hearts, whether we're following our own or falling in love with someone else's, play a huge role in our lives. Your heart, your emotions, your compassion, and your intuition all reside in the same place. In fact, if you ask a Chinese medicine practitioner to point to the area of the body where human *consciousness* lies, they will not point to the head, as Westerners would. They will point to the heart. It is from here, wisely, that the East teaches us to live.

In fact, the Eastern masters tell us that the heart is the "wisdom center," and if we listen, it guides us toward happiness, joy, and bliss. This isn't just Eastern esoteric thought, for the science of the heart has shown that the heart has its own neurological activity. There are some forty thousand neurons in the heart, with most of that neurological activity going from the heart to the brain. It's as if the heart were literally designed to communicate with the brain, whispering, "Listen to me; I have wisdom to share."

The heart's wisdom is different from that of the brain. The heart is nurturing, understanding, caring, supportive, forgiving, and full of love. So the heart and brain tend to take care of you in opposing ways. When these two wisdom centers are in sync, we feel aligned, powerful, and creative. Yet we've been conditioned to prioritize the brain over the heart, listening to our "thinking mind" over the sweet wisdom that resides in our chest.

So how do we access the guidance of the heart? The key to unlocking this center is slowing down. *Slow* signals relaxation, resting and digesting, balance, healing, integration, and, yes, the opening of the heart. It's the heart that puts us on the path toward joy, happiness, bliss, connection, and ecstatic experience.

Why, then, is the head prioritized? Simple answer: survival. When we are in survival mode, we use our marvelously pessimistic brains; we scan for danger, we try to predict it even when it isn't around, and we go looking for it in some future scenario. This gives rise to the monkey mind that we discussed in an earlier chapter as well as our inner critic, the inner oppressor. We all have an inner oppressor—those thoughts in our mind that are limiting and full of self-doubt, shame, blame, and self-loathing. It's the inner dialogue of "not good enough," "I can't," "not smart enough," "not pretty enough," "not handsome enough," "not important enough," or "I don't deserve it."

We all have negative self-talk that plays like a broken record. It's there for a reason: to keep us safe. It's there as protection because it wants our safety over our happiness. It chooses responsibility over love. And it's in direct conflict with the self that we truly want to live from.

In this chapter, we cover all kinds of heartfelt love, from self-love to love for friends, family, and colleagues to love and lust for romantic partners. Even if you're single, I highly recommend that you read the romantic and sexual sections of this chapter. Most, if not all, of the exercises can be used in company or in solitude.

Connection

The Self and Others

The first two pillars of slowness that you've learned so far cover your mind and body, the seat and the temple of your soul. This, for you as an individual, is life-changing. But until we can apply our newfound slowness and holistic healing to our hearts and our relationships, the pillars are incomplete. After all, it is our relationships that have the most influence over our hearts and, of course, our happiness. Many studies support this, indicating that the way we relate to ourselves and others and the quality of our connections dictate our level of life satisfaction more than anything else.[1]

While logic and safety have their place, the heart reigns supreme. It is love, it turns out, that is the most vital element to living our very best lives. Relationships are our playgrounds for expressing our love. And the best type of love is expressed with care and consciousness as well as, you've guessed it, *slowness*.

This inner critic is an important part of the tapestry of the self, but it doesn't need to rule all the other aspects of who we are. This inner critic has a place, but the inner critic desperately needs to be put in its place. The inner critic is hypervigilant, meaning it will take charge even when it's not needed. Because you are hardwired for survival, this part of the self likes to take center stage.

If you are interested in joy, love, happiness, peace, tranquility, bliss, and all the other feel-good emotions and states of being, you must get that inner critic in line. We have already learned techniques to help with this by slowing down the body, slowing down the breath, and slowing down the mind . . . but now what? When you slow down, there's an opportunity to invest your energy in other areas, like the heart. And when you put your attention, energy, and focus on the heart, a whole new world opens up.

Being more heart-centric might sound warm and fuzzy, but reorienting to the "feel-good" aspect of the heart can be scary, difficult, and unnerving. If it weren't, there would be a lot more people who are heartful—kind, compassionate, loving, and joyful as a primary way of being and moving through the world.

Before we dive into how to bring slowness into our relationships in the name of optimizing them, there is one person in particular whom you must love before anyone else. It's as RuPaul once said: "If you can't love yourself, how in the hell you gonna love somebody else?"[2]

Slow Self-Love

Do you love yourself? Can you forgive yourself? Can you be compassionate to yourself?

Many people recoil from these questions, worried that they might come across as narcissistic or powerless if they nod in affirmation. The truth of the matter is that self-love couldn't be further from narcissism and selfishness. Self-love is about your relationship with yourself. Selfishness is about what you can get from others, often without consideration of returning the favor. Self-love and being self-centric are vastly different.

The truth is that self-love is shrouded in ambiguity, as there is very little information on how to go about loving ourselves or figuring out which part of us is doing the loving and which part is receiving that love.

For many years, I confused self-love with a superficially similar yet profoundly different concept: self-care. Self-care is just a rudimentary step, the doorway to self-love. Self-care is akin to charging up your car, tuning up the engine, and making sure you have good directions and healthy snacks for the trip. Self-love is going on the journey. Self-love is the key that unlocks the treasure of happiness within.

Examples of self-care are eating well, exercising, sleeping well, hydrating, meditating, and going to therapy. Food, rest, water, and movement are often seen as the four pillars of self-care. All of these examples and more can be found in the "Slow Mind" and "Slow Body" sections of this book. All of this is foundational, but there is much more to 360° health than that. We need to build the rest of the beautiful temple of the self and not get stuck on the ground floor. You can take long bubble baths, play golf, get massages, do hot Yoga, take a Qi Gong class, swim in the ocean, go for a bike ride, hike in nature, get a facial, and many other activities to tend to yourself.

Self-care involves training the mind so that you can show up in your life as your friendliest self and therefore maintain vital connections. It involves lovingly applying sunscreen to your face to make sure you don't burn when you go out in the sun. It involves cozying up in a warm, fluffy sweater so you don't get cold in the winter. It involves taking a break from the grandkids to read for a while or do a sudoku to keep your intellect sharp. It involves asking your partner for a massage from time to time to loosen your lower back so that you can go to work the next day pain-free. I could go on for pages, but you get the idea.

As you can observe from these simple examples, without self-care, the vehicle that is your body and brain would cease to function optimally. Most people know this, and most people I have come across practice at least basic self-care to get by. But just because someone practices basic self-care and brushes their teeth before bed doesn't mean they actually *love* themselves.

Self-love goes beyond external action. Self-care is often something you can *see* someone do for themselves, whereas self-love is usually invisible to the untrained eye. True self-love is a profound and unwavering connection with yourself that has a level of solidity. By "solidity," I mean that your level of self-love doesn't waver depending on your achievements and failures. If the feeling you have toward yourself is completely dependent on whether you've checked off items on your to-do lists and whether you hit your career goals, this is not self-love. It is self-liking at best.

I know this because I experienced self-liking and self-loathing firsthand in my early sporting career. During my time in college, I was fortunate to be part of the prestigious UC Berkeley soccer team. Achieving this had always been a cherished dream, and the moment I was selected for the university, my excitement knew no bounds.

That was where my self-liking journey began. The opportunity to represent my school on the soccer field was a privilege I was determined to make the most of, and I was proud of myself. In moments like this, I liked my life and liked myself in the circumstances that I was creating.

That said, it wasn't all rainbows, good grades, and well-timed shots. There were plenty of difficult moments where I didn't make that pass or I missed that shot, where my grades dropped or I wrote a paper that was highly criticized. It was during these times that I noticed my own inner critic swell. The voice in my head was no longer an ally or a friend but rather a harsh, overbearing general. I'd punish myself internally when I failed to meet my expectations.

The dance between my self-liking and self-loathing came to a halt just before halftime in a home game against a rival school. I jumped up in the air to head the soccer ball, and an aggressive player from the other team took out my legs. I came crashing down, landing on my tailbone. The impact sent a bolt of excruciating pain through my spine and lower back. I hobbled up and tried to play for the next few minutes. The coach took me out of the game.

The euphoria of playing collegiate soccer gave way to frustration when that fateful soccer match led to a severe back injury. The team doctors gave me cortisone shots and painkillers. After a few days of Western medicine, my back pain was no better and the medication had given me a stomachache. My back hurt, I could barely walk, I was nauseated, and my mood was in the pits. I was walking around campus with my chin down and a grimace on my face. The team doctor told me I'd be out for the season.

All the progress I had made, all the confidence I had built up, came crashing down with that one crippling injury. As I watched my teammates continue to play, self-doubt and self-loathing began to creep in. I found myself questioning my worth beyond the soccer field—without the game, who was I?

In one particularly dark moment, I realized that I needed to confront my self-loathing head-on. I realized that I had built my identity around being a soccer player, and that identity had now been torn away. It was no wonder I was struggling, but it was time to accept my new body and my fallible self. It was time to rebuild, not as the athlete I had once been but as the person I could become.

It was then that I turned to Eastern medicine, meditation, and body therapies like Qi Gong, Tai Chi, and Yoga. I remembered a martial arts teacher of mine discussing the power of Qi shortly after crushing a stack of bricks with his bare fist. I was ten years old at the time and completely bewildered at how he had done it. Before he broke the stack of bricks, he had me hold and lightly punch one brick with my own hand. The brick was heavy and hard and hurt when I rapped my knuckles on it even lightly.

He explained that Qi, internal energy, was power and that power, when directed skillfully, could create amazing feats like breaking a stack of bricks. He then told the group that Qi could be used for healing and that the true power of energy was medicinal. After exploring Qi Gong and acupuncture, I was a whole new person. My pain had diminished considerably, and my mood was greatly improved. It was like a miracle—my body was responding positively, and the healing process had begun.

Qi Gong remains my passion to this day, and I have a lot to thank it for. But perhaps the most significant transformation came from learning to love and forgive myself. Through mindfulness practices and self-compassion, I gradually shifted my perspective. I realized that my self-worth shouldn't ever have been tied to my achievements and external goals. Over time, the journey from self-loathing to self-love became a tale of redemption. It wasn't an overnight process, nor was it always smooth sailing. There were setbacks, moments of doubt, and times when the past seemed to grip me tightly. But I kept pushing forward, reminding myself that I was not defined by my failures or my injuries. I wasn't even defined by my wins. What I chose to define myself by was the person I was, one with his heart in the right place. I was enough.

So I get it. It's easy to like ourselves when things are going well and when we're performing as we expect. It's even easier to like ourselves when other people do. But self-love is much bigger than this. Moreover, when you actually love yourself, external validation ceases to have as much importance as it did before. I, like many other people, enjoy compliments and positive reflections from others to this day. But it's important to view them as an added bonus to your already solid relationship with yourself rather than a lifeline.

Depending on external validation to gauge how much you are worth is a very dangerous game that can lead to chronic insecurity and toxic relationships. Those addicted to external validation are often easy to manipulate. It's also difficult to be in a relationship with someone who needs to be validated because they don't love themselves. If we don't love ourselves, we can become a bottomless pit of desire for love from others. This is highly frustrating for those we love, as no matter how much validation they give us, it will never be enough because nothing can replace the most important love of all, which is, of course, self-love. Without it, life is very challenging. If we don't love ourselves, we can't love life, or anything in it, on the deepest level.

As you can see, a lack of self-love can lead to dire consequences in our relationships with ourselves and others. But an abundance of it can lead to heaven on Earth.

Coming back to our original question now . . . what is self-love? If it's not self-care or self-liking or linked to personal achievements and validation from others . . . what is it?

Self-Love Defined

Self-love emerges from the inside, from a place of deep acceptance of ourselves as well as a solid base of compassion for who we are and how we think, act, and behave.

It involves embracing both the light and shadow aspects of our being and recognizing that imperfections and mistakes are integral parts of the human experience. It's a commitment to prioritizing your own well-being (that's where self-care comes in) in the knowledge that you deserve to be happy and that your happiness is just as important as everyone else's. Self-love is nurturing a positive inner dialogue with yourself and speaking to yourself in the same conscious, kind way you would speak to a beloved friend.

Genuine self-love is rooted not in ego or self-centeredness but rather in a harmonious alignment of thoughts, feelings, and actions that honor your authenticity. *Authenticity.* This is an incredible part of the process, for when you love yourself, you give yourself permission to be authentic, to be true to yourself. That is, with a base of self-love, you're no longer afraid to be yourself for fear of what others may think of you.

Self-love also involves setting healthy boundaries that protect you against self-neglect and external toxicity from others who may cross your path. This makes room for genuine connections to flourish because once you love yourself, you have a resilient sense of self-worth that isn't dependent on those external circumstances I mentioned earlier. That's not to say that once you love yourself, you completely give up on bettering yourself. On the contrary, self-love leads to a gentle inner calling to continually seek personal evolution driven by an innate understanding that being our best, happiest, healthiest, most successful selves is a prerequisite for contributing positively to the world.

At its core, self-love is akin to self-peace. No matter what may be happening on our planet, in our countries, neighborhoods, offices, and homes, or on the inside, there is tranquility. On the inside, there is a safe space.

Exercise #17: Heartfulness

Here we move from mindfulness to "heartfulness." This is where we actually get to practice self-love and take the concept from a theoretical approach and understanding to an actual experience. Go to qigo.ng/slow for a free version of this exercise.

1. Start by getting comfortable, either sitting in a chair or lying in a comfortable position.
2. Bring a subtle smile to your face by gently lifting the corners of your mouth and bringing a smiling energy to your eyes.
3. As you inhale, accentuate the smile on your face. Make it big, almost like posing for a picture.
4. As you exhale, melt that smile on your face into your heart. Bring that feel-good positive energy inside and let it rest in your heart.
5. Imagine that your heart is shining with golden radiance and bright light. (If you have difficulty visualizing, imagine a sunset that you've actually experienced and just bring that sensation into your heart.)
6. Keep going. Inhale and bring a big smile to your face. Exhale to relax your face and feel your heart smiling, glowing golden.
7. Think about a few things that you appreciate about yourself. Let this gratitude shine inwardly.

8. Recall a few moments of deep appreciation in your life—being out in nature, having a conversation with a good friend, a good laugh, or anything that elevates your heart.
9. Let the love, light, and radiance build in your heart.
10. Breathe slowly and deeply.
11. Let your heart tune in to the frequency of love.
12. Allow that love to shine through your whole body.

Now that we know what self-love is (and isn't), it's time to cultivate it actively. We live in a world that constantly reminds us of what we lack and what makes us "not enough." Add trauma to that, and we've got a lot of people with serious self-worth and insecurity issues. It's a lot to unpack, and I understand that if you've done no prior self-love work or had little support from your parents or guardians in building up your self-esteem, the idea of loving yourself out of the blue may seem out of reach. I'd like to reassure you, however, that this isn't the case. Self-love starts at home. It starts with you, and you alone. And it starts in front of the mirror.

Exercise #18: Mirror Work

The exercise you're about to do was given to me by my therapist in my darkest hour. This practice is simple yet throws you right into the deep end of self-love. For me, it's been the fastest, most authentic way to build self-love from the inside, from absolute zero.

Begin by setting aside just a few minutes and placing yourself in front of a mirror. Any mirror will do. As you look into your own eyes, become mindful of what thoughts may pop up in your head, especially the negative ones. As you look into the mirror, say aloud, "Even though this may be hard, uncomfortable, and unfamiliar, I choose to love myself anyway."

At this point, many people experience an emotional response. For more people than you may think, this mirror work will be the first time they actually witness themselves. It may trigger feelings of vulnerability. And that's okay. Keep going. As you continue to look yourself in the eye, you'll say the following sentences:

"Today, I choose to forgive myself for . . ."

"Today, I choose to be proud of myself for . . ."

"Today, I choose to deem myself worthy of . . ."

"Today, I choose to love myself because . . ."

Take a deep breath between each sentence, saying it slowly and with intention. You can expand on each point to deepen the value of the message you're sending yourself. Here's an example of what this might look like:

"Today, I choose to forgive myself for all the mistakes I made in my romantic relationships and for hurting [INSERT PERSON]. Everyone makes mistakes, and although I'm not perfect, I'm a good person and deserve my own forgiveness now."

Slow, deep breath in and out.

"Today, I choose to be proud of myself for not giving up when things got really tough at work last week. I was brave and strong and practiced self-care. I deserve to celebrate my wins now."

Slow, deep breath in and out.

"Today, I choose to deem myself worthy of gifts and compliments from other people. It's my birthday today, and I deserve to receive love from others."

Slow, deep breath in and out.

"Today, I choose to love myself because, quite simply, I need my own love more than I need anyone else's. I deserve to treat myself with the same tenderness with which I'd treat an innocent child."

I recommend that you take the time to do this every morning for 30 days and see what happens. I have a friend who even does all of this while brushing her teeth, morning and night! This exercise takes only a couple of minutes, but its effects are profound. And the effects don't just happen while you're doing this activity. They also happen out in the real world. Little by little, you'll start to see that the way you speak to yourself in your head, begins to change. Little by little, you'll catch yourself for calling yourself "stupid," and begin to speak to yourself with more care.

Little by little, you'll begin to notice when others don't treat you with respect because your level of self-worth will rise. Little by little, you'll start receiving from others, not just giving to them. Little by little, you'll begin to judge yourself less harshly and see yourself as a beloved friend rather than your own worst enemy.

It's from this place, once you love yourself truly, madly, and deeply, that you can expand that love and share it with someone else.

QUICK MYTH: Self-love is selfish. There are more important things to do with our time than learning to love ourselves.

SLOW REALITY: Self-love is the foundation for all the other relationships in our life. If we want healthy minds, bodies, and connections with others, self-love is the foundation.

Cultivating Slow, Deep Connections with Others

You might be wondering how a book on slowing down will help you relate to others. Not only is it helpful, but it is also essential to clear communication, conflict resolution, and deeply intimate experiences, both emotional and sexual. As with everything else in this book, I want to show you how going slower gets you more of what you want.

Self-love is a wonderful foundation for developing loving, intimate relationships with others. Relationships are complex, ever shifting and dynamic, swirling with external life experiences, and evolving as each individual grows and changes. I want to give you some tools and resources that can truly help cultivate sweetness and the positive exchange of energy in your relationships.

From this newfound foundation of self-love, you'll grow your compassion outward to envelop all your loved ones with the same acceptance, understanding, and forgiveness for not being perfect. Although I noted earlier that our relationships have the greatest impact on our happiness, relationships also have the greatest impact on our stress levels. If you're like most of us, when you reflect on the most difficult, stressful times in your life, a relationship will probably bubble up to the surface of your memory.

This is completely normal. According to the Mental Health Foundation, recent studies from Ireland and the United States have shown that negative social interactions and relationships, especially with romantic partners, increase the risk of depression, anxiety, and even suicidal thoughts. That said, positive, love-filled connections reduce the risk of these issues.[1]

Additionally, research has shown that couples who are in love experience a dramatic boost in their immune systems. Let that sink in . . . falling in love is good for your physical health, as healthy as consistent exercise and good nutrition.

We'll dive into romantic, sexual connections toward the end of this chapter, but the section you're about to read can be applied to any kind of personal relationship, including friends, family, and colleagues.

When we bring slowness into our relationships, what we're essentially bringing is mindfulness and a deeper awareness. And when we bring mindfulness into our relationships, that's where true connection happens.

Have you ever connected deeply with someone while at the movie theater? Did you and the person sitting close to you experience profound romance with all the fireworks or deep, nourishing platonic conversation while watching *Fast & Furious 8*? My guess is NO because you were focusing on something else. This is an extreme example, I know, but sadly, it seems that many of us have our own movie streaming in the background of our minds while we're relating to our loved ones. Although we may set Saturday afternoon aside for "quality time," many of us struggle to be truly present with the person we're with. But it's in those moments of presence that love is cultivated, nurtured, and preserved. That's where mindfulness comes in, which leads us to a very simple exercise that you can practice the next time you're speaking to someone or simply sharing your space with another person.

Exercise #19: Slow Down Conflict

Conflict, hurt feelings, poor communication, agitated words, snappy comments, and lashing out wreak havoc on relationships with our loved ones. If there is one important takeaway from this section, it is to slow down before engaging in conversation when there is stress or tension in the relationship dynamic.

The majority of our relationship problems stem from urgency, the feeling that we must respond right away while we are feeling agitated. This is normal. Most people do it. We get upset because someone we love isn't showing up in the way they are "supposed" to. And you need to let them know, right now, that they aren't being the person you expect them to be. I mean, if people just did what we wanted, when we wanted, all the time, life would be so easy!

Alas, people have their own minds, their own rhythms, and their own ways of moving through the world. Even your children. Realizing that you don't control your children is a difficult hurdle to overcome. Just because you want them to eat that healthy piece of broccoli doesn't mean they will. Just because you want them to go to sleep at 7:30 pm doesn't mean they will. Just because you planned the perfect birthday party doesn't mean they won't be upset when they have too much sugar and stimulation and another kid at the party starts playing with one of their new toys.

I witnessed this last example firsthand. My kids were at an eight-year-old's birthday party. The parents had gone all out for the party. Lots of cake, candy, games, presents, and activities. The kids were having a blast. The birthday girl was having the time of her life . . . until one of the children took an open present and started playing with it.

The birthday girl was in terrible turmoil, exclaiming, "Give it back; it's mine!"

The other little girl pulled away and continued playing with it. The mom of the birthday girl tried to reason with her: "Honey, you can share, you have lots of presents here to play with."

"No, it's mine. It's my present. It's my birthday!" the birthday girl said, now yelling.

"You should be grateful," said the mom in a harsh tone. "Look at all these presents you have."

"I want that one!" she yelled again, tears welling up in her eyes.

"Do you want me to take away all your presents?" the mom said with a raised voice that all the other parents could hear.

"No!" the little girl screamed loudly.

"That's it! Go to your room!" the mom yelled back. "I'm going to tell your father about this."

The little girl stormed off to her room, crying. Her sobbing could be heard throughout the house. But after a few minutes, the crying subsided into quiet whimpers. After a few more minutes, it had stopped.

Then the dad went into her room. I could hear, and so could everyone else, Dad parentally and very logically going through the details of what had transpired throughout the day: "We spent lots of money on this party, had all your friends over. Your mother has been planning this for weeks, and now you are acting like a spoiled little brat. You need to apologize to your mother or we will take away your presents."

"No!" The little girl started crying again. She was hysterical at this point. Dad came out of the room shaking his head, apologizing to his friends. He was an acquaintance of mine, and I asked if he was open to a suggestion. He replied, "Please, anything to help." I told him to just give the situation some space and to slow everything down.

I told him that I imagined what he wanted was for both his little girl and his wife to be happy and have fun. He nodded. I told him that the day wasn't ruined and that in about fifteen minutes, all would most likely be well and back to fun. He looked at me and said, "How?"

I told him to let his little girl have about fifteen minutes on her own. I explained that her nervous system was hijacked, she was overstimulated and stressed, and that the nervous system needs fifteen to twenty minutes to come back to baseline. I told him that she was almost there when he went into her room and retriggered her. The same was true for his wife. It's stressful when your child throws a tantrum in front of guests. In those moments, parents want their kids to just do, act, and even feel what they are told. No amount of logic will help kids get over an emotional surge. Only slowing down, giving it a little time, and not saying or doing something that adds fuel to the emotional fire will work.

After ten minutes, the little girl came out of her room, eyes red but with no more tears. Dad asked if she felt better. She nodded. He apologized for threatening to take away her toys. She apologized for yelling. He asked if she would apologize to Mom. She nodded and immediately went over to the couch where her mom was sitting and gave her a hug. The party continued. Everyone had fun, especially the birthday girl.

This type of circumstance happens in all of our relations. We add triggers on top of triggers when we are upset. The first trigger for the birthday girl was another girl playing with her toy. At that moment, the birthday girl had a stress response. When you witness someone in a stress response, here's the magic... slow down. Slow down your reaction, slow down before responding, slow down before saying anything. If you feel that someone else's stress is stressing you out, slow down.

The best way to deal with these situations is not to do anything... yet. I've had to remind myself of this many times as a parent. When I use it, every time, I think, "No way, it worked!"

"Do nothing, accomplish everything," as the Taoists say, worked well one early afternoon at Whole Foods.

There I was with my twins, three years old at the time, when a tantrum erupted over who was to get the purple pack of bunny gummies on aisle 3. Neither one of them wanted the red pack; they both wanted purple. They cried. I said, "Bunny gummies are right here in my pocket until you feel better." They cried louder. I didn't react or engage. What I did was practice slow breathing. I waited. I could feel my embarrassment as people looked at two crying kids in a grocery cart. I smiled. I breathed. I did this for five minutes. Five really long minutes. By minute six, they were done. No more tears, no more sobs, no more "I want bunny gummies." They had forgotten all about the purple pack. In fact, they were laughing about something else (they were throwing fruit into the air from the cart and I was catching it, pretending to be upset). They were playing with each other and the produce in the cart. Kids are impulsive, in the moment, and highly emotional. They can switch from sadness to joy in the blink of an eye. Just let them without interference.

I've seen parents lose it when kids act out. I've witnessed parents yelling at their kids to stop being so loud. I've seen parents spanking their kids after a little one hit another kid, saying "No hitting!" before spanking them again. If you are behaving the same way as your child and yelling at them to stop the very thing you are doing, they won't get the message. Why do parents do this? Because they are in stress mode. Logic, reasoning, and rational behavior go out the window when we are stressed. Your best self goes on the shelf, and your aggressive self takes center stage. This is when we do things we regret or that hurt the people we care most about.

When you are upset, stressed out, or emotionally off-center, slow down. Wait. Don't react or respond.

Do your slow practices. Start with slow breathing. Use the slow mind. Practice slow body movements (go to another room or even a bathroom stall and practice for even two minutes).

After this, you will be in a much better position to communicate, ask for what you need, hold a clear boundary, say no with compassion, or apologize sincerely.

This works for parents and kids, and it works especially well in romantic relationships. Couples tend to lash out, get defensive, and take out frustrations on each other because they act when they are stressed. Slow down. Notice when emotions are running high, sense stress in your body—tightness in the chest, clenching in the belly, contraction in the neck and shoulders—take a slow break, and do not engage in conversation. Gently and respectfully tell your partner that you need just a few minutes by yourself so that you can show up as your best self for them. This way, they're less likely to be triggered by you leaving the room. Wait, breathe, shake it out, and come back to a much clearer conversation with far better results.

Exercise #20: Mindful Relating

This exercise is intended to be done in secret. Don't tell the person you're practicing with what you're doing, as their behavior may change.

The next person you happen to be in front of will be your first experiment! Whether it's your husband, wife, partner, child, friend, or colleague, this is where we create a mindful playground of connection using all of your senses.

Start by seeing the person in front of you. Don't just notice they're there; actually *look* at them. Take in what they're wearing, the colors of the fabrics, and how the texture contrasts with the smoothness of their skin. See the ever-changing expressions on their face as they communicate with you or perhaps just go about their business. Notice the subtle details, the subtle beauty, about them that you might usually overlook. Observe their body language. Are they fidgeting? Are they making eye contact? Are their gestures emphasizing certain points?

Now truly listen to what they say as you engage in conversation. Listen not just to respond but to truly understand what they're saying. Set aside your own mental chatter and be present with each and every word. Notice their accent, the volume of their words, and how they express themselves. Appreciate them as you witness them fully.

If you can, and if it's appropriate, bring some gentle touch into the exercise. If the other person agrees, give them a hug. Feel the warmth of their embrace and take a deep breath to bring your awareness to the way they smell (try not to do this in a creepy way!). Make this embrace precious, appreciating that the other person is offering you their affection. If a hug isn't possible, you can simply touch their hand or the top of their arm, allowing the microembrace to occupy your full attention. If even that sort of touch is risky for the context, then with all the warmth you can muster, connect with that person energetically through eye contact that emanates kindness.

As you practice this exercise with the different people in your life, you might notice a deeper level of connection forming. By being fully present and engaged, you allow yourself to feel a true connection and show the other person that you value and respect their presence. This can lead to more meaningful interactions and stronger relationships over time.

Remember, mindfulness takes practice, so don't be discouraged if it feels challenging at first. As you continue to cultivate this skill, you'll likely find that your relationships become richer and more fulfilling.

Slow Communication

This brings us nicely to slow, conscious communication. Nowadays, our communication is often instantaneous yet distracted and therefore surface level. In a world brimming with notifications, emojis, and abbreviated phrases, the art of deep and deliberate conversation is fast being forgotten. That's why we're bringing slowness back.

These days, time has become a precious currency. When you dedicate time to conversing with a fellow human being, you're offering a heartfelt investment that is an investment well made. Unhurried discussions lead to authentic, meaningful discussions—the only ones worth having! So whether it's during a leisurely walk, over a shared meal, or even in the office, allow yourself to set aside enough time to connect with whomever you're talking to. It is essential to practice conscious, unhurried, and deliberate communication with your loved ones, but it can even be practiced with acquaintances or strangers. I don't know anyone on planet Earth who would complain that they've been listened to, understood, and communicated with too well!

Slow communication starts with mindfulness, of course, which we covered in the previous section. Now you can imagine your conversations as a dance; instead of becoming totally lost in the rhythm of your own head, you're focusing on the person in front of you, flowing with their every move. Put your mental playlist on pause, and immerse yourself in the melody of their voice. When your partner, friend, or stranger speaks, become an attentive audience of one. Set aside your urge to jump in with advice or anecdotes, and don't interrupt.

This part is important. Embrace the natural silences. Give them the same quiet, loving space you would want if you were expressing something close to your heart. Allow their words to paint a vivid picture in your mind, and look them in the eyes as much as you can. Tune in to their feelings, their struggles, and their joys. Let your reactions be a canvas on which they can express themselves fully.

This is what is known as "active listening," and it's crucial for excellent communication. To take it even further, you can try paraphrasing what your friend, family member, or colleague is saying, followed by putting yourself in their shoes. For example, say a loved one is struggling to juggle work and family life. He's complaining about it, telling you he's on the brink of burnout. You may listen until he feels that he's said everything he wants to say, followed by a genuine response such as "I feel you, bro. It sounds like you're really stretched right now and feel like you're on the brink of burnout. I'm sorry to hear that. If I were in your shoes I'd probably be feeling lonely and disappointed that I wasn't getting the help I need. Is there anything I can do to support you?"

Active listening doesn't come easy to everyone, and when you have your own stuff going on, or perhaps a strong opinion opposing what you're hearing, it can be a challenge to clear your mind and just *listen*. If you find yourself swimming upstream when it comes to processing what your speaker is saying, try repeating their sentences silently in your head in real time. That way, you ensure that you've taken in what you've heard.

When we feel heard, we deepen our love for the listener. So once you start listening properly, be prepared for people to fall in love with you!

Active listening inevitably enhances your empathy within your personal relationships, and it can also give you a unique edge at work. Recent research from the University of Southern California has revealed that poor listening habits and skills affect more than 70 percent of all employees in the United States, resulting in suboptimal performance, more mistakes, misunderstandings, missed opportunities, arguments, and unstable professional relationships.[1] Can you imagine what would happen if all of us actually learned to listen? The benefits would be endless for both our personal and professional lives.

That said, there's one missing piece of the puzzle when it comes to slow, conscious, meaningful communication, and that is, of course, when it's your turn to express yourself. How you do this is of paramount importance.

Here, we're training ourselves out of "word vomiting."

"Word vomiting" is that moment when words just spill out without any metaphorical brakes. It's when you're talking or writing and everything comes rushing out in a chaotic frenzy. Imagine a whirlwind of thoughts, ideas, and information being thrown out without much order or care for how others are catching it. It's like a conversation tornado, where someone might be blurting out words at top speed, not even stopping to take a breath or think about what they're saying. The result is a mental mess—a jumble of words that can be all over the place. It's like trying to catch confetti in a windstorm—challenging and sometimes even overwhelming for anyone trying to keep up.

It's not just you in this conversation, remember. In front of you is another person with their own universe inside their head. Before you open your mouth to speak, ask yourself, "How can I express myself in a way that makes it easy for the other person to understand?" Conscious communication is not just about the words you choose; rather, it's about weaving a tapestry of emotions and thoughts in a way that resonates with the other on a profound level. So slow down and take a few moments to gather your thoughts and your resources before you dive in and speak.

And when you do, try to speak from your heart, not just your head. Doing this will take a certain amount of vulnerability and therefore courage. In one of my favorite books, *Daring Greatly*, Brené Brown describes vulnerability as "uncertainty, risk, and emotional exposure."[2] Contrary to popular belief, vulnerability does not equal weakness. Vulnerability comes with immense courage as we shakily step out of our comfort zone, put our hearts on the line, and take the risk of not being accepted by whomever we're expressing ourselves to. There is a risk that we won't be understood or will be judged. This is what makes expressing our truth a vulnerable experience. That said, vulnerability is akin to sunlight, illuminating the corners of our soul and creating a bridge between hearts. It takes vulnerability to forge deep, meaningful communication, and it takes deep, meaningful communication for love and compassion to grow. Therefore, it is the highest priority when it comes to our relationships!

A Note on Conflict

I hear you: "This is all well and good if you're conversing with Mother Teresa. But what if you're neck-deep in an argument or debate with someone who isn't following the rules?"

So here's a note on conflict. First, conflict is a natural part of any relationship. It doesn't have to be seen as a sign from the universe that your relationship is on the brink of extinction. In fact, it doesn't have to disrupt your connection at all. Conflict, when approached consciously, can provide fertile ground for even deeper connection, bonding, and insights. All you have to do is face your conflicts with the same mindfulness that you bring to other, more pleasant conversations, as learned above. Easier said than done, I know.

When disagreements arise, try not to let strong, short-term emotions steer the ship; let reason and empathy be your compass. Actively listen with an open heart, even when it's hard and even when the other person forgets their manners. Speak with respect, even when you're passionate about proving them wrong because they're just as convinced they're in the right as you are! Focus on solutions rather than the problem. Remember, conflicts are golden opportunities for growth, but it takes one person to rise above the pettiness and set a tone of love. Let it be you.

This all happens when we slow down, move out of stress, relax, and enter into heartfulness and mindfulness. From here, conversations become productive, forgiveness is accessible, and intimacy becomes inevitable.

> **QUICK MYTH:** Conflict is inevitable, so we might as well express our anger and let the argument unfold right away to get it over and done with.
>
> **SLOW REALITY:** When it comes to anger, it pays to go slow. Taking 10 minutes to calm down before engaging in an emotionally charged conversation may save a lot of time and heartache for yourself and the person you care about.

Exercise #21: Conscious Communication Boot Camp

As we've learned, conscious and slow communication is an art, a dance, and a symphony of hearts connecting. It requires practice, patience, and willingness to be fully present. Through deliberate conversations, you're sharing not just words but pieces of your soul. So it's now time to practice.

For the next three days, you will set the intention of bringing the Slow Principles into each of your interactions. Whether it's your spouse, friend, colleague, or bus driver, you will bring some intentionality into your interactions. First, assess which kind of interaction you're about to have. Is it casual? Formal? Is it a safe space to be vulnerable or a pleasant space for short, kind exchanges?

Next, bring in mindfulness, followed by active listening, followed by conscious speaking. I'll walk you through some examples from a theoretical day in my life.

Interaction 1: My Children (Close Relationship)

It's Monday, and it's time to get the kids ready for school. When I see them, I look them in the eye and say a genuine "Good morning, sweethearts" before serving breakfast. Over the breakfast table, I really witness my kids: I look at them, I notice their facial expressions, I notice the clothes they're wearing. I ask open questions like "What's happening at school today?" and listen. I listen to the words they say, but I also pick up how they're feeling and offer a safe space. When it's my turn to speak or express myself, I do so with love and respect (even when I'm rushing them out the door).

Interaction 2: My Tea Barista (Acquaintance)

After taking my kids to school, I head to my local tea house (the one I told you about in the "Slow Mind" section). I approach my tea barista and look him in the eye, truly witnessing and appreciating his presence. I ask him how he is, and I listen to the answer. He says he's "fascinated." Such a unique response! I tell him this and offer a paraphrase to show that I've taken in what he's said: "It's refreshing to hear you're in awe this morning! What are you fascinated by?" We have a brief conversation before he serves me my tea and I express my gratitude to him.

Interaction 3: My Work Partner (Professional)

Then it's time to hop on a video call with my editor. I put my tea to one side and open my laptop. Even though my editor is all the way in England, I set the intention of having a meaningful conversation. And even though our allotted time slot is only 30 minutes, I've set aside 45 minutes so that we don't have to rush or leave anything unsaid. I notice she's had a haircut, and I tell her how much I like it. She thanks me, and I notice her face light up with the compliment. She proceeds with the meeting. As she reports our progress with my book launch, I listen without interrupting, even though I have questions. When she has completed her report, I ask my questions in a clear, concise, and kind way that I know she'll understand. We dance between active listening and speaking from the heart and end the conversation with a warm "Thank you."

Interaction 4: My Qi Gong Group (Friends)

In the afternoon, it's time to record a training session with my Qi Gong gang. We've known each other for years, and we often enjoy Qi Gong retreats together. When I see them, I immediately greet them with a warm hug, feeling their embrace mindfully. I look them in the eye as I say hi and ask them how they are. I listen to their answers, but I also "listen between the lines." One of my friends comments that it was their birthday over the weekend, but "somebody forgot." That somebody was me. Although she's laughing when she says it, I feel a little bit of hurt behind the words. Once I know that she isn't going to say anything else, I tell her, while placing my hand on her shoulder, that I'm sorry I forgot her birthday. I told her that if I was in her shoes, I'd feel frustrated because we've known each other for so many years, and how could I be so forgetful? I express some vulnerability and tell her that I feel quite ashamed for missing her birthday and worried that she may think badly of me. I ask if I can treat her to a special dinner after our Qi Gong class at her favorite restaurant to make up for it, and I take action by putting her birthday in my calendar on my phone to repeat every year so I don't forget. She seems pleased by this and assures me that it's fine before we flow into the Qi Gong class. I witness my dear friends and students flowing gracefully through the movements, and I allow myself to rejoice in how peaceful their facial expressions are.

Now it's your turn. For the next three days, keep a journal where you'll write about your interactions. Focus on where you brought in mindfulness, active listening, and heartfelt, vulnerable self-expression.

Slow Intimacy

When it comes to relationships, one particular type of relationship tends to reign supreme in our list of priorities, for better or for worse. This beautiful form of love can make us or break us, fill us with passion and fill us with fear, bring stability to chaos or chaos to stability. It's the type of love that society allows us to obsess over because society is obsessed with it too. This type of relationship makes an appearance in the majority of our songs, movies, books, and histories.

It is, of course, the romantic relationship. And what makes a romantic relationship different from all of our other ones? *Intimacy*.

Marvin Gaye fans, the time has come. It's time to get some sexual healing.

This chapter will explore intimacy from the "slow" perspective, giving you techniques and tools to deepen intimacy. Slowing down has the potential to bring more pleasure, increase loving connection, and heighten orgasmic pleasure.

Does this mean that every intimate exchange needs to be slow and take a long time? Remember, going slow does not mean taking a long time. It means creating powerful moments, heightening energy, being conscious, and becoming heartful. It's about rhythm, exchange, variety, and timing. Slowing down during intimacy is another tool to help you live the life of your dreams, to truly connect to your romantic and intimate partnerships.

We often have a viewpoint of sexual intimacy from movies and other forms of entertainment. The slamming against the wall as the couple barely make it through the front door, the sex happening quickly while standing against the wall in the hallway, clothes barely pushed aside, in a panting quick exchange of pleasure is not the only way to deep romance, folks. In fact, this type of connection is probably one of the most uncomfortable and unsatisfying.

I'm not saying that this movie-type intimacy is bad if the time and the mood are right, but I am offering another way of connecting in a deep, rich, playful, conscious, and satisfying way that is sustainable and highly repeatable over and over again.

Sex, contrary to what many of our religions, dogmas, and cultures would have us believe, is a beautiful, sacred part of being a healthy human being. However, it's important to recognize that some individuals may identify as asexual or experience sexual dysfunction, and in such instances, some of the content of this chapter may not directly apply.

That said, sex has been found to boost the immune system, lower blood pressure, lower the risk of heart attack, lessen pain, improve sleep, and make people fitter.[1] But that's not all, folks. There's much more. Among the countless studies proving the miraculous benefits of physical intimacy, one has shown that having sex on a regular basis also makes you look ten years younger than people who are celibate! Why? Researcher Dr. David Joseph Weeks of the Royal Edinburgh Hospital claims that this is due to the triggering of "feel-good" chemicals combined with a human growth hormone that helps those who have sex retain a youthful complexion. Combine this with a racing heart rate, which boosts circulation and the flow of vital nutrients to the skin, and you've got yourself a fool-proof, pleasurable cocktail for vitality.[2]

To reap the benefits of intimacy, you don't have to engage in wild sex that throws you outside your comfort zone, nor is there any pressure to assume acrobatic positions. Penetrative intercourse isn't a prerequisite. As long as the loving, sensual, physical touch is present, the magic can begin.

The knowledge and wisdom of old that surrounded the mind-blowing benefits of sexuality was kept secret for thousands of years in ancient China, reserved only for the emperor and his closest circle. It was believed that these sacred teachings held immense power, not only in maintaining physical vitality and longevity but also in attaining spiritual enlightenment.

Taoist practitioners saw sexual energy as *divine* energy, Buddha nature, or universal creative energy. The coming together of two people in a physical sexual union was seen as an extremely potent force, capable of being harnessed and transformed into immense personal power, creativity, hyperoptimized health, and deep spiritual wisdom. This process was aligned with the broader principles of Taoism, which emphasize balance, harmony, and the interconnectedness of all things.

Within the imperial court, three specialized female Taoist advisers were tasked with imparting these secret teachings to the emperor himself. These advisers were chosen for their deep understanding of both the philosophical and practical aspects of Taoism as well as their ability to guide the emperor in the intricate art of harnessing sexual energy. These teachings were considered essential for the ruler's health and well-being as well as the prosperity of the empire.

The preservation of these teachings as secrets had multiple motivations. First, they aimed to maintain the exclusivity of the emperor's power and influence, as possessing the knowledge of these sexual practices bestowed a unique form of authority. Second, the secrecy surrounding these practices was likely a protective measure to prevent the misuse or misunderstanding of such powerful energy cultivation techniques. The potential for misinterpretation or exploitation could have been considered a risk to both individual practitioners and the stability of the empire.

As history progressed and dynasties changed, the secrecy surrounding these teachings began to erode. With the decline of imperial power and the opening up of Chinese society, some of the once exclusive teachings started to be shared among broader circles. This dissemination allowed certain aspects of Taoist sexual practices to become more widely known. In the West, however, they remained mostly unexplored until recently.

From multiple orgasms to skyrocketing levels of authentic connection and pure, divine love, the world of deeper intimacy awaits you. I recorded an audio program on it, called *Taoist Sexual Secrets*, with my business partner, Rachel Abrams. So if you're interested in diving deeper into the "how-to" side of things that goes beyond what I can offer you in this book, feel free to give it a listen.

But for now, I'll give you the basics.

Before we dive in, I'd like to take a moment to address readers with sexual trauma. If you have experienced sexual trauma, I suggest that you take extra care when practicing the following exercises. If you begin to feel at all uncomfortable or unsafe while practicing, I urge you to seek advice and support from a therapist who specializes in sexual trauma. Creating a safe and comfortable environment, both physically and emotionally, is essential for a positive and healthy sexual experience.

And now, a note for my nonbinary and transgender readers: a profound aspect of the Taoist teachings that you're about to learn is that all humans contain a mixture of both masculine and feminine energies. Depending on your unique sexuality and gender identification, you may find that your energies are more masculine, more feminine, or a balanced mix of both. Your erogenous zones and your relationship with them may differ from what is described below too. All of this is okay, and it may be worth taking the time to explore yourself and your sexuality in a safe way and a safe environment to better understand your own truth.

Taoist Sexual Secrets

The first step toward conscious, slow, authentic intimacy is to ignite your arousal. By "your," I mean both your and your partner's arousal. What turns us on varies considerably, and I'm not here to judge what floats your boat. What's important is that the energy of arousal is flowing through your body. In Taoism, this energy is known as "Jing Qi," a fundamental life-force energy (Qi) that is born from sexuality and arousal. It is often associated with both sexual fluids (such as semen and vaginal secretions) and the deeper energy underlying them.

Taoist philosophy views Jing Qi as a precious resource that should be conserved, cultivated, and worked with to support overall health, vitality, and spiritual growth. It is nothing to be ashamed of. On the contrary, Taoism teaches that this energy is the highest form of human pleasure and a gateway to enlightenment.

The way to activate, circulate, and cultivate Jing Qi for the greatest possible benefit and pleasure is to slow down. Think about it: why are we being intimate with our partners? Is it to have a baby? Yes, on rare occasions. Nonetheless, we are being intimate to connect, to get a rush of feel-good internal chemistry cocktails, to exchange heart energy (hence the term "making love"), and to feel the powerful orgasmic energy of bliss course through us. This happens maximally if we allow sexual energy to build, exchange, circulate, and flow. This happens when we go slow.

Building arousal occurs in very different ways for male and female energies. In general, male sexuality is described as akin to fire and feminine sexuality to water. That is, male sexual energy is quick to get hot and quick to blow out. Female sexual energy, on the other hand, much like water, is slow to heat up and slow to cool back down. This explains why men generally tend to access states of arousal faster than women, and women tend to last longer in the state of arousal than men even after orgasm. Additionally, in Taoist philosophy, female sexual energy starts in the head and flows down to the heart, then to the genitals. This links strongly with the Western notion that the brain is the biggest sexual organ.

Male sexuality, on the other hand, experiences the opposite. According to the Taoist teachings, male sexuality begins in the genitals and moves up to the heart, then to the head.

It is also said that men, or more masculine people in general, need to have sex to feel love, whereas women, or more feminine people, need to feel love to have sex.

If you're in a partnership where the levels of arousal are very distinct, don't fret. Just because your partner builds Jing Qi in a different way than you doesn't mean the quality of the sex will be diminished. It just means that you're about to have lots of fun learning how to turn them on in the way that they love the most. For women, this generally means taking things slowly, creating a safe, warm, comfortable space, and engaging in nonpenetrative, pleasurable activities such as massage, light touching, kissing, and perhaps talking sensually to build the Jing Qi to the same level as that of the more typically masculine partner.

Once both parties have their Jing Qi flowing, sex can unfold from a place of deep desire. When we slow down, we allow feelings of substance to arise within us, such as care, compassion, and love, as opposed to pure lust.

Before you engage in any sexual activity, such as direct touching of the breasts and genitals, oral sex, or penetration, set the goal of pleasure. *Pleasure*, not orgasm. Having an orgasm as your end goal takes away your level of mindful pleasure in the moment, often leading to pressure, anxiety, and disappointment. Orgasms are great and have a host of health benefits, but it doesn't mean that they should be treated as the sole purpose of sex. Paradoxically, when we let go of the pressure and intention to have an orgasm, taking our focus off the end goal and into the moment, that's when an orgasm is most likely to occur.

The most efficient way to deepen pleasure is to slow down the whole sexual encounter. This doesn't mean that a romantic sexual interlude needs to take hours. It simply means to go slower and allow energy to build and pleasure to expand.

So as we engage in sexual activity with our partner, we're coming from a foundation of Jing Qi, we've removed the end goal of an orgasm, and we're also going *slowly*. The slower you go, the more steady the building of Jing Qi will be. As we've come to learn in this book, the slow overcomes the fast in countless ways. Why would you finish off a piece of chocolate cake in ten seconds when you can take pleasure in it for ten minutes? Why would you rush through your wedding, your birthday, or your Christmas celebrations? The same goes for sex. Make it an event.

Slow Sexual Courtship

There's an unfolding energetic process to sexual intimacy. There's a beautiful alchemy that can happen in the space between meeting someone and having physical sexual intercourse. That space can be taken slowly so that energy and pleasure build up. Sexual alchemy is the process of mixing together different elements and energy and coming up with a heightened, more refined expression of that energy. Take the loving energy of the heart and combine it with the orgasmic sexual energy of the genitals, and you have a deeply powerful alchemical elixir.

The energy of love and sexual energy is what many of us are seeking. Whether we are listening to good music, reading a romantic novel, watching a movie, or having a candlelight dinner with our partner, we are seeking some combination of these two energies.

How do we excavate the treasures of love and sex? First, you guessed it, go slow. These energies need tending to and are easily disrupted (remember that stress in the body and mind will be prioritized over love and sexual intimacy).

As in cooking a good meal, certain ingredients need to be combined at the right time. The fire, the heat, the amount of time, as well as what ingredients and when those ingredients are combined, all contribute to the flavor of the meal. In the same way, being intimate with someone can be brought together with different timing, different activities, and different recipes for the perfect experience.

To truly bring out the fullest capacities of the loving heart and the blissful sexual energy, going slow is a great way to entice these energies through the relationship. What do we humans do as courtship? Hopefully, we talk first! We often meet someone, go on a date, and have a good conversation. Speaking is the first path to the heart. In fact, in Chinese medicine, the tongue (not in terms of taste but in terms of speech) is known as the flower of the opening heart. We talk to feel our way into someone's heart energy as well as to get to know the quality of their mind.

If all goes well, the alchemy progresses, and we might kiss. The lips and tongue, again, are related to the heart. Kissing is a way to feel into someone's energy and to sense the alchemy of the heart, the way in which our heart connects to their heart, more deeply. Kissing is a way to nonverbally communicate heart to heart.

Why do we kiss? Have you ever thought about it? When you kiss someone when you truly resonate with them from heart to heart, it feels amazing, feels uplifting, and opens the heart to joy and bliss that you weren't experiencing moments before. We do not kiss to exchange saliva; we kiss to share intimacy or, in other words, to exchange heart energy.

Once this heart energy is exchanged, the pathway to the genitals opens up. The energy descends or cascades downward, and the energy of sexual arousal opens up. The energy of a loving, awakened heart combined with arousal and orgasmic blissful energy is one of the sweetest elixirs of life. Taoists recommend lingering in this pristine energy for as long as possible. This can mean more caressing, more conversation, and not having sex for days, weeks, or longer, depending on how much time you are spending together.

In partners who are already sexually active together, whether it's been weeks or years, the same applies . . . go slow. Taking time before sexual intercourse to caress, converse, play, and open up different erogenous zones can be a great way to create a deep, powerful alchemy.

This brings us to what to actually do with your bed partner between the sheets. In Taoist sexual philosophy, as mentioned before, we work with Jing Qi energy as a pathway to health, enlightenment, and spiritual wisdom. This involves converting our Jing Qi, aka our arousal, into Qi, or life-force energy. This energy can be stored in our bodies for healing, power, and manifestation and, of course, shared.

Exercise #22: Energy Exchange

Note: This can be done with new romantic interests or long-term partners after kissing and before sexual intercourse as a way of slowing down to exchange energy. Go to qigo.ng/slow for a free version of this exercise.

1. Stand facing your partner, your palms facing down, their palms facing up. Put your hands over each other's without touching.
2. Take some slow, deep breaths through the nose.
3. Feel the energy passing like a current between the hands. The hands, like the tongue, are another expression of the heart. In fact, the heart meridian goes right through the palms of the hands.
4. Do this for a few minutes.
5. Switch so that your hands are facing up and their hands are facing down over yours without touching.
6. Feel the energy coursing between the palms.
7. After a few minutes, talk to your partner about how it felt to be close without any physical touch.

Exercise #23: Sexual Reflexology

One of my first jobs out of college was to help write books for the Qi Gong master Mantak Chia in Thailand. One morning in the dining hall, just after morning Qi Gong stretches and flows, Master Chia came up to me with a worn and tattered bunch of pages stapled together. He said, "This is the next book to work on." I looked down at the manual and it read, *Sexual Reflexology*. My first thought was "And I'm getting paid for this?"

Sexual Reflexology had many components. First, it described the way in which Taoist masters diagnosed the energy of couples to determine whether they were compatible. This worked for arranged marriages as well as marriages of choice. The Taoist master considered facial features, hands, hair, and body composition to read various energetic qualities and give feedback to couples about how to increase compatibility and connection.

Another aspect of this ancient manual was using sex as medicine. If someone had lower-back pain, the Chinese medicine doctor might prescribe a sexual position for the couple that would direct energy to that particular energy system for healing. If someone had asthma, they would prescribe a different sexual position for the lungs. This was known as healing through pleasure.

Another aspect of sexual reflexology was pressure-point and massage therapy. The manual described how different pressure points lit up or circulated energy to the sexual organs for increased pleasure, arousal, and exchange of energy. So who wants to learn some pressure points to turn on your partner?

Slowing down the sexual experience might include some sensual pressure-point therapy.

Have your partner lie down on the bed, a massage table, or the floor. Make sure the room is at a comfortable temperature and they can relax. Feel free to set the mood with some candles and relaxing music if it suits the situation.

The lower legs are a great place to start since there are many points that move energy through the sexual center.

Begin by taking one foot in each hand. Gently squeeze the arches, soles, toes, and ankles to relax them. Next, start to find those therapeutic pressure points. I will give you guidelines on how to find those points, but don't worry too much about getting them exactly right. Even if you aren't on the exact right point, you are still doing your partner some good. The most important thing is loving intention, tuning in to your partner's energy, and connecting.

Stimulating acupressure points can be done in a variety of ways. You can press and hold a point. You can press, release, press, release over and over on the point. You can press and circle, or you can press and wiggle on the point.

Touch is the highest form of communication. It transcends words, content, and context in a language your body understands. When we touch, we express our emotions directly. When you place your hands on someone, feel a sense of loving kindness in your heart and whatever you do will come across as a positive, elevating exchange of energy.

Point 1: Three Yin Meeting Point (Spleen 6)

To locate the Three Yin Meeting Point, known as Spleen 6 in Chinese medicine, place four fingers on your inner ankle bone, called the medial malleolus. The point is between the shin bone and the muscle. Use your thumb to press and circle on the point. It's usually a little tender or sensitive. You can move up and down the leg to find the point. Ask your partner if they can feel the energy or the sensation of the point. Check in with them about the pressure, asking if they would like more or less. Sometimes these points ache or hurt with very little pressure, so be conscientious about what feels good to them.

This point is good for increasing libido and bringing calm, relaxing energy to the sexual center. Spleen 6 is also therapeutic for menopause symptoms, calming the mind, improving sleep, deepening relaxation, and balancing hormones.

Point 2: Supreme Stream (Kidney 3)

Kidney 3 is on the inside of the Achilles tendon (the tendon at the back of the leg that connects to your heel). The point is in the depression between the inner ankle bone and that tendon. Kidney 3 is "the source point" on the kidney meridian, which means that there is a lot of energy available here. In Chinese medicine, the kidneys control Jing Qi, or sexual energy. Anytime you enhance the kidney energy, you are improving sexual energy circulation, hormone balance, and libido. You can massage both points on both feet at the same time, just as with Spleen 6. Place your thumbs on the points, massaging them in a circular motion or just holding them with firm pressure.

Point 3: Bubbling Springs (Kidney 1)

Kidney 1 is located on the bottom of the foot near the ball of the big toe, just slightly inward toward the midline of the foot. It's easiest to find by curling the toes and finding the deepest indentation near the ball of the big toe but slightly more inward. Kidney 1 is a very relaxing pressure point used for anxiety, one that induces deep relaxation. If we wish to cultivate sexual energy, clearing stress is essential. Stress is the destroyer of sexual intimacy. Whatever clears and relieves stress will naturally allow the body to relax and sexual energy to be more easily accessible. Put both thumbs on Kidney 1 on both feet. Alternate pressing the points on both feet simultaneously—left, right, left, right with pressure that suits your partner.

Point 4: Heart Meridians Through the Arms and Hands

The arms and hands have many pressure points to help relax and open your partner for connection. The heart meridian (energy channel) runs through the inside of the arms to the palms of the hands. By massaging the hands, you help open the heart for deeper, more loving intimacy with your partner.

Start by taking your partner's hand in yours. With both thumbs, press and squeeze their palms. Notice the texture, the temperature, and the quality of their hands. Each person's hand tells a story of their life. See if you can get a glimpse into your partner's.

Point 4.1: Heart Palace (Heart 8)

The heart meridian starts in the armpit area and runs down the inside of the arm through the palm of the hand to the pinkie. If you curl your pinkie down to the palm of your hand, it will land on Heart 8. This point clears anxiety and stress and benefits the physical health of the heart. Press and release a few times, then press and circle on the point. Ask your partner how it feels, if they want more pressure or less.

Point 4.2: Spirit Gate (Heart 7)

To find Heart 7, have the palm face up and massage the crease of the wrist in line with the pinkie just on the inside of the little bone that sticks out slightly. That bone is called the pisiform (that's a fun word to say, isn't it?). Heart 7 opens the heart for deeper connection and is used for relaxation, improved sleep, and clearing anxiety.

Point 4.3: Palace of Toll (Pericardium 8)

Physiologically, the pericardium is the sac around the heart that helps the heart stay cool and prevents it from overheating. Energetically, the pericardium protects the heart. Think of the pericardium as the emotional immune system. Its job is to keep negative emotional energy out and allow positive emotional energy in. By stimulating the pressure point, we facilitate this process. Locate the point by having the person curl their middle finger inward toward the palm. The point is where the middle finger touches the palm. Take your thumb and press and release the point for 30 seconds to 1 minute. Then press and circle.

Point 4.4: Inner Gate (Pericardium 6)

Pericardium 6 has lots of uses in Chinese medicine. It is used for many things, including nausea, seasickness, motion sickness, and morning sickness. It helps relax the stomach and ease the nervous system.

It's also good for emotional protection, clearing anxiety, and letting go of emotional stress from other people. Its location is three fingers' width from the crease of the wrist. Find it by having your partner place three fingers on the crease of their wrist and massage beneath it. The point is between the tendons in the very center of the wrist. Press and release, press and wiggle, or press and circle.

It's always a great idea to ask your partner for feedback when massaging any of these points. Each and every body is different, and your partner may prefer a lighter touch or more pressure. See which of these points has the most effect on them, and ask if they would like you to continue touching them there or whether they'd like you to move on to a new point. Communication is key.

Exercise #24: Microcosmic Orbit Breathing

This practice is designed to convert your arousal energy, Jing, into Qi to enhance your sexual pleasure and romantic connection and store it for healing and well-being. We do this by slowly breathing through the meridian (energy channel) the Taoists call the "Microcosmic Orbit."

In this practice, energy moves up the spine as we inhale over the top of the head and descends down the front of the body as we exhale. Regardless of whether you have a partner to do this with, start by practicing the breathing technique alone.

Bring your attention to your genitals, and as you do, bring to mind a scene from the past when your arousal was high. Bring vivid images into your mind, building your arousal. You may choose to lay a hand over your genitals as you do so or even touch yourself. Once you are aroused, begin by inhaling deeply and imagining energy running from your genitals all the way up your spine and to the top of the head. As you do so, clench your pelvic floor muscle (also known as the pubococcygeus [PC] muscle) as if you're pumping energy from your genitals to the top of your head as you inhale. (It's the same muscle you'd pull in if you were stopping a stream of urine from flowing.)

As you exhale, relax your pelvic floor and imagine the energy running from the top of your head all the way back down into your genitals. Repeat the process again and again, circulating your Jing Qi throughout your body, up the spine as you inhale and down the front of your body through your heart, stomach, and gut as you exhale.

By building strength in the PC muscle, you prepare your body for stronger, more intense sensations of pleasure and orgasm. And by circulating your energy from the genitals, you spread your Jing Qi all over the body, increasing your overall Qi. Go to qigo.ng/slow for a free version of this exercise.

Exercise #25: Fusing Jing Qi with a Partner

Once you've mastered Microcosmic Orbit Breathing, you're ready to engage in sexual activity with a partner.

In this exercise, we begin by sitting in front of our partner and looking lovingly into their eyes, breathing deeply. From here, bring your hands out in front of you and hover your palms over one another. Bring your left palm over their right palm and your right palm under their left palm. Bring your palms about three inches apart, and feel the energy there.

As you hold the energy between your hands, imagine that you're sending beautiful golden light from your head down into your heart. Feel deep gratitude toward your partner. Now let the loving, golden energy in the heart drop down through your arms and to your hands, sending this energy into your partner's palms.

Once you're connecting with this loving energy, begin to connect to your Jing Qi, your sexual energy, in your genitals. Without touching your partner, begin to draw this sexual energy up from the genitals on the inhale by squeezing that PC muscle and drawing it up to your head, just as you did before on your own. This time, on the exhale, drop the energy down to your heart center, down the arms, and into your partner's palms.

Here, you're combining loving heart energy with Jing Qi from your genitals, fusing love and arousal and exchanging this energy through your hands. Try breathing in unison as you draw sexual energy up from your genitals and exhale it down into your palms.

There is no pressure to engage in lovemaking, but this exercise is a great doorway to it if it feels authentic and if both partners' Jing Qi levels are flowing strongly. If you'd like to continue the practice and deepen it with physical intimacy, maintain the breathing as much as you can throughout. Ensure that the intimacy is slow; take ample time to gently touch and kiss the erogenous zones before touching or licking the genitals—or, as they say in Taoism, before the Jade Stalk enters the Hidden Palace!

Some erogenous zones are

- The earlobes
- The hands and fingers
- The insides of the wrists
- The backs of the knees
- The tailbone
- The feet
- The scalp
- The nape of the neck
- The pubic hairline
- The perineum (the area between the testicles and anus)

As you transition to touching the genitals, make sure to do so slowly and gently. This is especially true for what the Taoists call the Precious Pearl (clitoris) and the Hidden Palace (vagina) as well as the Bells of Love (breasts). It is also true for the Jade Stalk (penis) and the Dragon Pearls (testicles). These names may make you laugh (as I did when I first read them), but the Taoists did know a thing or two about bringing slowness, beauty, and sacredness to lovemaking, including the way they referred to the sexual organs. They also referred to sexual acts in poetic ways, such as "sipping from the vast spring" and "blowing the flute." I'll let you figure out what those mean!

Remember, the goal of the practice is to exchange, heighten, and increase pleasure and circulate orgasmic energy. While you are making love, go slow. Push the goal of orgasm to a distance and bring the goal of pleasure to the moment. As orgasmic energy increases, slow down and bring in some other techniques. For example, do some slow breathing in unison. Hold each other close, look into each other's eyes, and breathe. Try to match your breathing rhythm with your partner's, inhaling or exhaling in unison. This will allow your energy to settle, flow together, and circulate. Doing this for just 1 minute can heighten pleasure and allow orgasmic energy to circulate between you. Do this multiple times for multiple energetic orgasms.

> **QUICK MYTH:** The goal of sex is the climax. A physical orgasm is the only way both parties will feel satisfied, and hopefully, it won't take too long!
>
> **SLOW REALITY:** Sex can be a magical, otherworldly experience and an opportunity to connect on a profound level with the person to whom we're making love. Sex should be experienced as a journey rather than a destination, although various forms of climax, including energetic orgasms, may be enjoyed.

What's Love Got to Do with It?

When it comes to our relationships, there should always be time for love. And for love to flourish, slowness and presence are vital.

As we've learned, this love starts with ourselves. In fact, the Taoists taught that within us are three treasures: the Jing Qi (you now know what that is!), Qi (life-force energy), and Shen Qi (the energy of the spirit). These are interconnected energies that we need in order to live fulfilling, healthy lives. The biggest mistake many of us make is searching for those energies outside ourselves. But the reality is that they are *already* inside us. And they're waiting for us to tap into their power.

Once you've gained mastery over your own energy, a true energetic union with someone else becomes possible. From a space of self-love and empowerment, we can truly show up for other people, whether it be our spouse or our bus driver, as our best, most centered, most authentic selves. From this foundation of love, we can love and connect with others on a whole other level. Self-love's influence extends beyond the realm of romantic affiliations too, weaving its way into every facet of our engagement with life.

And why wouldn't we take the time to do this? When we slow down and think about it, isn't love what it's all about?

If you ask me, a life experienced from the heart is one that's well lived. And if love is all we've achieved by the time we find ourselves on our deathbeds, that will be more than enough.

Principles Unite

YOUR SLOW DAILY ROUTINE

> In pursuit of knowledge,
> every day something is added.
> In the practice of the Tao,
> every day something is dropped.
>
> —Lao Tzu, Tao Te Ching, Verse 48

You've now read through the three pillars of slowness: Slow Mind, Slow Body, and Slow Relationships. You're aware of why they are vital to living your healthiest, happiest life, and you have the science to prove it. You're motivated by the vast advantages of slowing down, knowing that it's the only way to be present for your own experience of life as well as for your loved ones.

Now it's time to slow down and bring it all together.

The musician who practices diligently can transform a mere sequence of notes on a page into a symphony that stirs emotions in the masses. The athlete who trains methodically can convert raw talent and strategic training into victorious performances on the field.

The scientist who experiments tenaciously can turn abstract hypotheses into groundbreaking discoveries that change the world.

Your daily slow practice will serve as the key to unlocking the true benefits of the treasure chest of knowledge you've learned in this book. Through daily practice, ideas take shape, create tangible experiences, and eventually become part of who you are.

Your Slow Daily Routine

The following is an example of how you can incorporate the exercises you've learned in this book into your daily routine. It will take you from morning all the way into the night, covering breathing techniques, meditation, movement, self-love, mindful relating, stress reduction, slow eating, connecting with nature, and conscious intimacy. Although that's a long list of slow exercises, you'll be surprised at how little time they take and how you can integrate them into habits you already have.

That said, take what serves, leave what doesn't, and make it your own! Let's begin.

07:00 – Slow Breathing
Based on Principle 2, Slow Body:

- Exercise #13: The 5.5 Breathing Rule
- Exercise #15: Go Fast to Go Slow Breathing
- Exercise #16: Getting Friendly with Your Nasal Passages

Wake up and dive into one of the three breathing rituals of your choice: Go Fast to Go Slow Breathing (Wim Hof style, great for bringing more alertness to the brain), Alternate-Nostril Breathing (breathing in through one nostril and out the other, great for anxiety), or the simple 5.5 Breathing Rule (breathing rhythmically in for 5.5 seconds and out for 5.5 seconds), great for setting your slow breathing tone for the rest of the day. You don't have to practice these for long. Some of my Slow Community members practice for just a couple of minutes as soon as they open their eyes, and others prefer a deeper 10-minute session.

If you'd like to revisit the more detailed instructions on how to practice these breathing techniques, please refer to the "Slow Body" section for "The Breath as Medicine: Taking Your Vitamin O."

07:10 – Slow Meditation
Based on Principle 1, Slow Mind:

- Exercise #4: The "Where Am I?" Meditation

After breathing deeply and slowly, begin your "Where Am I?" meditation sitting up in bed. Ask yourself quietly, "Where am I?" before scanning your environment and becoming more present. Respond aloud, "I am here." Sense and feel where "here" is. Notice the sounds in the room. Notice what surrounds you. Notice the sensations on the surface of your body. Keep repeating the question and answer as you scan your body from the top of your head down to your face, neck, and shoulders: "Where am I?" "I am here."

If you'd like to revisit the more detailed instructions on how to practice this meditation, please refer to the "Slow Mind" section for an introduction to mindfulness meditation.

07:20 – Slow Movement
Based on Principle 2, Slow Body:

- Exercise #6: The "Go Slow, Enter the Flow" Qi Gong Sequence
- Exercise #7: Qi Break: Spinal-Cord Breathing

Get out of bed and begin with a simple Qi Gong practice, starting with the "Go Slow, Enter the Flow" exercise. Stand with your feet shoulder-width apart with your knees just slightly bent before inhaling and slowly raising your arms to shoulder height. Your elbows should be fairly straight. You can imagine that you have strings gently pulling your wrists upward. Exhale and float your arms back down slowly. Repeat these movements, inhaling your arms up and exhaling them down. Think of your arms as the waves of the ocean, and feel the element of water within you.

Do this 10–20 times before commencing your Spinal-Cord Breathing. As you take a deep breath in, reach your arms up to the sky, then imagine pulling an imaginary barbell weight slowly down to the tops of your shoulders. Bend your spine backward and look up at the ceiling to encourage an opening in the chest space. As you exhale, curl your spine inward and bring your arms down, hands touching centrally in fists, all the way to your groin area so that you can fold yourself into a little ball. Inhale and reach your arms up toward the sky again, opening up your chest, bending backward, and pulling down that imaginary barbell. Repeat this process of expansion and contraction 10–20 times.

If you'd like to revisit the more detailed instructions on how to perform these exercises, please refer to the "Slow Body" section for "Channeling Your Inner Bruce Lee."

07:30 – Slow Tea/Coffee

Based on Principle 1, Slow Mind:

- Exercise #2: The Mindful Tea Ritual

Head to the kitchen in a leisurely manner, and make your morning cup of tea or coffee. Prepare it slowly and mindfully. No phones, podcasts, or loud music with lyrics just yet. Once your beverage of choice is prepared, drink it slowly without doing anything else. Take a few minutes to smell, feel, and sip with full awareness. Notice the texture, taste, and temperature in your mouth. Follow the comforting sensation down the throat and into the belly. Take a deep breath, and then do it again. Notice how you feel throughout the process.

If you'd like to revisit the section on slow rituals when it comes to beverages, please refer to the "Slow Mind" section for "Welcome to the Mindful Tea Shop."

08:00 – Slow Self-Love
Based on Principle 3, Slow Relationships:

- Exercise #18: Mirror Work

After breakfast, head to the bathroom to brush your teeth. But before you do, take a few minutes to look at yourself in the mirror. As you look into your own eyes, say aloud,

"Today, I choose to forgive myself for . . ."

"Today, I choose to be proud of myself for . . ."

"Today, I choose to deem myself worthy of . . ."

"Today, I choose to love myself because . . ."

If you're really pressed for time, you can actually do this while brushing your teeth . . . although your voice will sound kind of funny. Toothpasty mirror work is better than no mirror work!

If you'd like to revisit the more detailed instructions on how to practice this mirror work in the best way, please refer to the "Slow Relationships" section for "Slow Self-Love."

09:00 – Slow Relating
Based on Principle 3, Slow Relationships:

- Exercise #20: Mindful Relating

As soon as you arrive at your place of work/responsibility, notice the people around you, using your mindfulness skills to connect with them with full conscious awareness. Take in the subtle details, the subtle beauty about them that you might usually overlook. Observe their body language. As you greet them, if you feel comfortable, make some eye contact. When it comes time to converse, truly listen to what they say as you engage in the conversation. Listen not just to respond but to truly understand what they're saying. Actively listen. When it's your turn to respond, speak with consciousness and compassion.

If you'd like to revisit the more detailed instructions on how to practice slow relating, please refer to the "Slow Relationships" section for "Cultivating Slow, Deep Connections with Others."

11:00 – Slow Qi Break
Based on Principle 2, Slow Body:

- Exercise #7: Qi Break: Spinal-Cord Breathing

and Principle 1, Slow Mind:

- Exercise #1: First Aid for Stress: Primal Shaking

If you have a couple of minutes for a Qi break, take a moment to stand up, leaving your desk behind you and easing any tension in your back. Take this opportunity to connect to a slow, deep inhale and exhale while engaging in your Spinal-Cord Breathing technique (the same one you practiced this morning). As you bend your spine backward, open your chest space, and as you curl in, allow a closing in the front of your body. If you've experienced any stress during the morning, consider taking yourself off to a private place to engage in some Primal Shaking. Notice the stress in your body. Where are you feeling it? What symptoms are you experiencing? Take a deep breath in, and as you exhale, imagine blowing out the tension the stress has caused. Take another deep breath. This time, on the exhale, begin shaking your entire body the way your dog shakes after a bath.

Now be still and return to your breath. Return to slowness. Return to your center. Return to your desk.

If you'd like to revisit the more detailed instructions on how to practice Spinal-Cord Breathing, see "If You Are Forced to Sit on Your Butt All Day" in the "Slow Body" section. For more information on Primal Shaking for stress release, please refer to the "Slow Mind" section for Exercise #1: First Aid for Stress: Primal Shaking.

13:00 – Slow Lunch

Based on Principle 2, Slow Body:

- Exercise #9: The 32-Second Chew Rule
- Exercise #10: Mealtime Mindfulness
- Exercise #12: Acupressure for Optimal Digestion

Leave your desk and go to your favorite place to eat lunch. Resist the urge to use your phone or look at any screens while you eat. Take a second to gaze lovingly at your food. Take a sniff . . . what aromas can you smell? Take a deep breath before taking your first bite. Notice the flavors, textures, and temperature of your food, chewing thoroughly (32 times, remember?) and enjoying the experience. Is it delicious? Allow yourself to let out an "Mmmmm."

Put down your knife and fork between bites, and slowly eat your meal. If you can eat with someone else, even better! That way, you'll be talking as well as eating, which will slow down the process even more. Take pleasure in your slow lunch break and finish your meal.

Now, for optimal digestion, locate the Stomach 36 point for a short acupressure boost. This point is located four finger widths down from the bottom of your kneecap, along the outer boundary of your shin bone. Massage the area in small circles or tap it with all your fingers gathered together for optimal precision. Massage or tap with pressure for 30 seconds.

If you'd like to revisit the more detailed instructions on how to practice slow eating, please refer to the "Slow Body" section for the 32-Second Chew Rule and Acupressure for Optimal Digestion.

17:00 – Slow Nature
Based on Principle 2, Slow Body:

- Exercise #8: Slow Down with Nature's Big Five

After work, carve out about 30 minutes to get out in nature. Whether it's at your local beach, forest, mountain, park, or garden, if it's natural, it'll do! As you walk around outside, if you can, take off your shoes and socks to ground yourself to the earth on the grass, soil, or sand. If there are trees around, imagine that you're breathing with them as you walk by. Notice the colors and fragrances of nature. If you prefer, you can take a swim. Watch the sun go down if your time zone and cloud cover allow it. Whatever you do, connect with Mother Earth at this time.

If you'd like to revisit the more detailed instructions on how to connect with nature, please refer to the "Slow Body" section for "Why It's Time for You to Go 'Au Naturel.'"

18:30 – Slow Dinner
Based on Principle 2, Slow Body:

- Exercise #9: The 32-Second Chew Rule
- Exercise #10: Mealtime Mindfulness
- Exercise #12: Acupressure for Optimal Digestion

and Principle 3, Slow Relationships:

- Exercise #20: Mindful Relating

Here, as you eat, draw on your mindfulness skills just as you did at lunch. Eat your dinner slowly. If you're eating with family or friends, make sure to balance your mindfulness between your food and *them*. Actively listen to them as they speak, noticing every detail of their body language and showing them that you care about their words. Inquire about their day, and listen for their emotions as well as the content of what they're saying. Ask how they're enjoying the meal, and express your gratitude for the meal too. Combine mindful eating with mindful relating.

If you'd like to revisit the more detailed instructions on how to practice slow eating, please refer to the "Slow Body" section for The 32-Second Chew Rule and the "Slow Relationships" section for "Cultivating Slow, Deep Connections with Others."

21:00 – Slow Intimacy
Based on Principle 3, Slow Relationships:

- Exercise #22: Energy Exchange
- Exercise #23: Sexual Reflexology
- Exercise #24: Microcosmic Orbit Breathing
- Exercise #25: Fusing Jing Qi with a Partner

Whether or not you have a partner to practice with, this is your time for slow intimacy.

Begin by practicing your Microcosmic Orbit Breathing. If you're alone, focus your attention on your genitals and recall a past arousing moment. Picture vivid scenes to intensify arousal. You may choose to touch yourself with love and care if desired. Once aroused, inhale deeply, envisioning Jing Qi energy rising from your genitals to your head. Tighten your PC muscle as you inhale, as if pumping energy upward. Exhale, releasing the pelvic floor, and imagine energy flowing from head to genitals. Repeat, circulating Jing Qi: inhale up the spine, exhale down the front, enhancing pleasure and energy throughout your body. Treat this as your self-care and self-love time.

If you're with a partner, begin by gazing lovingly at them while exchanging Jing Qi and loving heart energy through the hands, palms hovering above one another, about 3 inches apart. Do this as you practice your Microcosmic Orbit Breathing. Connect with your sexual energy without touching at first, but then, if desired, commence physical touch. For deeper intimacy, maintain your breath as you explore, taking time for erogenous zones. As Taoism teaches, proceed gently and slowly before any kind of intercourse. Enjoy this time for slow intimacy.

If you'd like to revisit the more detailed instructions on how to go about slow intimacy, please refer to the "Slow Relationships" section from Exercise #21, Conscious Communication Boot Camp, to "What's Love Got to Do with It?"

22:20 – Slow Gratitude
Based on Principle 1, Slow Mind:

- A Thank-You Note
- Exercise #3: Gratitude Meditation

Before you allow yourself to drift off to sleep, take a moment to reflect on what you're grateful for. You may choose to close your eyes and meditate on this or bring out your journal to write a list. Ponder all the blessings in your life, the comfort of your home, the luxury of your belongings, the incredible people who show you love, the qualities within yourself that you're grateful for, and the opportunity to have lived another day on this planet. See this as the gift it is.

If you'd like to revisit the more detailed instructions on how to practice gratitude, please refer to the "Slow Mind" section from "A Thank-You Note" to Exercise #3: Gratitude Meditation.

22:30 – Slow Bedtime Breathing
Based on Principle 2, Slow Body:

- Exercise #14: Vagal Breathing: The Breath of Joy

As you lie down to go to sleep, commence the Vagal Breathing technique for enhanced relaxation, placing a hand on your belly. Breathe in for the count of 4, feeling your diaphragm move your belly outward, then hold your breath for 2 seconds before breathing out for the count of 8, feeling your belly deflate and relax back in. Repeat until you fall asleep naturally.

If you'd like to revisit the more detailed instructions on how to practice Vagal Breathing, please refer to the "Slow Body" section for Exercise #14: Vagal Breathing: The Breath of Joy.

Creating Your Daily Slow Routine

Take a moment to reflect on a typical day for you. Which exercises can you seamlessly fit into your schedule? Take out a pen and a piece of paper and plan your slow day tomorrow, integrating as many practices as possible.

- Slow Breathing
- Slow Meditation
- Slow Movement
- Slow Tea/Coffee
- Slow Self-Love
- Slow Relating
- Slow Qi Break
- Slow Lunch
- Slow Nature
- Slow Dinner
- Slow Intimacy
- Slow Gratitude
- Slow Bedtime Breathing

Perhaps you prefer to exercise in the afternoon or make love in the morning. Maybe you take your dog out first thing, so you wish to connect with nature before rather than after work. All this is fine. Make your routine work for you. Make it as easy as possible to stick to, and set small, achievable goals. Before you know it, all these activities will become sturdy habits that are an absolute pleasure to carry out.

Give it a go, then do it again the next day, the day after that, and the day after that. Notice how you feel. In a month's time, schedule 30 minutes in your calendar to write in your journal about your experience, noting any insights or additions for the upcoming slow month. Make adjustments when needed. Make it work. After all, slow, deliberate months make up a year. Slow, deliberate years make up a decade. And slow, deliberate decades make up a slow, deliberate life.

Just sit back, relax, and watch the results unfold, slowly but surely.

The Slow Life

Closing Words

> The soft overcomes the hard.
> The slow overcomes the fast.
> Let your workings remain a mystery.
> Just show people the results.
>
> —Lao Tzu, Tao Te Ching, Verse 36

In closing, I'd like to share a familiar fable. In a time long ago, a story unfolded—a tale that, after reading this book, is likely to resonate with you more deeply than before.

Once upon a time, in a sunlit glade, there was a hare, as swift as the cheetah and as cunning as the fox. This hare unashamedly boasted of his speed and grace to all who would listen. The toads and the hornbills rolled their eyes as he rambled on about his ability to outrun the most terrifying predators. The deer avoided him. The warthogs fell asleep during his many monologues. Only one animal entertained his outbursts of pride: the tortoise.

The tortoise was known by all the animals for her steadfast nature and embrace of the rhythm of life. On the other side of the watering hole, this calm tortoise lived as unhurriedly as the flow of the nearby streams. From across the water, the tortoise listened in silence to all the hare had to say until one fateful day, with a tranquil smile on her face, the tortoise challenged him to a race.

"A race!" declared the hare in disbelief. "Against an animal as slow as you?"

The tortoise nodded earnestly. "Yes, sir. To the baobab tree on the other side of the forest."

The hare, brimming with overconfidence, accepted the challenge with a dismissive laugh. The forest creatures gathered to witness the race, anticipation hanging in the African air like mist.

The morning sun sent its golden rays through the trees, casting long shadows upon the racecourse, which had been lovingly laid down by the spider monkeys. It was time for the race to begin. As the eagle cry signaled "Go," the hare dashed forward, a streak of lightning through the foliage. His tiny heart pounded to the rhythm of his thudding paws, and the cheering of the bonobos spurred him on. He couldn't see a thing as he ran, but he didn't care. He was greedily lapping up the praise as he pressed forward, full steam ahead.

Meanwhile, the tortoise embarked on her journey, each step measured and deliberate. Her eyes were fixed on the path ahead, undistracted by the crowd's cheers.

As the hare raced on, the thrill of his speed inspired him to pause and rest beneath a shady acacia tree. As his small, fluffy chest heaved, the hare closed his eyes, confident that his victory was assured. In contrast, the tortoise moved on, her pace unyielding, slow, and strong.

Minutes turned to hours, and the hare awoke with a start, panic seizing his heart. He immediately sprinted once more, with no time to warm up. His initial swiftness had transformed into exhaustion, and his muscles shook with fatigue. The finish line loomed, and the tortoise, ever the steady traveler, was almost there.

Tension hung in the air as the many animals of the forest watched the tortoise make her way to the baobab-tree finish line, cheering loudly and with disbelief. In the final moments, as the tortoise crossed the finish line with a last gentle step, a hush fell over the forest. A few seconds later, the once boastful hare finally arrived, gasping and defeated. "No!" he cried. "No! How can this possibly be?"

The tortoise turned to him with compassion. "My friend, slow and steady wins the race."

There is much to be learned from this old fable. The slow prevails over the swift, the consistent over the erratic. The tortoise was triumphant not merely because of her pace but due to her enduring determination, humility, and focus. "The Tortoise and the Hare" is a timeless reminder that in life's great race, it is not always the swiftest who reach the finish line first. And now, after completing this book, you know why.

At the beginning of this chapter, you read a quotation. Those of you with a keen eye and an above-average memory may have noticed that this timeless quotation from the Tao Te Ching is the very same quotation that led off the introduction to this book.

Now, however, you understand it on a whole new level. In a world obsessed with speed and instant gratification, the notion that the slow can outpace the fast might have sounded radical before you understood the three Slow Principles. And as you go out into the world far beyond the comforting touch of this book, there will be those who don't believe this could be true. In this case, as the Tao Te Ching taught us thousands of years ago, and as the fable "The Tortoise and the Hare" confirmed, speed will lead us down the wrong path. It is time to be the slow change you wish to see in the world. No need to preach, "just show people the results." Results, after all, cannot be argued with.

Show them how joyful, calm, and clear your mind can be when you slow down, breathe, meditate, and practice mindfulness. Show them how healthy, fit, and strong your body can be when you move slowly, eat slowly, and connect with nature. Show them how deep, meaningful, and passionate your relationships can be when you first love yourself and then love others in the slow, conscious way they deserve.

Slow down to unlock your happiness, friends. Slow down to awaken infinite peace within you, and slow down to wake up to the beauty and wonder that is this life. The moment to begin is now.

Tomorrow is not guaranteed. Today is all we have, and all we ever will have.

Slow down enough to experience it.

Acknowledgments

I started writing *Slow* on a trip with a good friend, the author Doug Abrams, to Maui in 2015. This book, like a good wine or brick of pu-erh tea, has been ripening *slowly* over some years. And here it is *ready* to be consumed, deliciously, by you, reader.

I'd first like to acknowledge my appreciation to you for picking up this book. My students and my audience have inspired me to learn, grow, and articulate these teachings for some thirty-five years now and become the person I am today. So thank you.

Acknowledgments are a form of appreciation. Writing this section has filled me with tremendous gratitude for so many people—mentors, students, and family. I want to thank Doug for his mentorship, insights, and expertise, but mostly for all the laughter we've shared over the years.

It has been a wonderful and *slow* process getting this book finished and published. Since its conception, this book has taken many journeys, coming to fruition over some ten years. As my good friend Daniel Ray Villegas told me, "There's Slow, and then there's too ssssllllooowwww." Thanks, Dray, for helping this book move at just the right pace. Dray was instrumental in key areas of the book, like the title, always chiming in with key phrases and wordsmithing.

I want to thank my editor Amy White for her incredible tenacity, focus, clarity, and brilliance. She has made this book shine and made the difficult parts of writing a book joyful and fun.

I'd like to thank my Holden Qi Gong team for supporting me in my mission to bring ancient wisdom to modern life. Thank you, Ben, Chen, Jackson, Jared, Kevin, and Vinny. I'd especially like to thank Jenny and Todd for their support, collaboration, and dedication.

Thank you, Tami Simon and Sounds True, for such a talented team, founded on integrity and spiritual wisdom.

I want to thank my daughters, Lainey, Maile, Kyla, and Harper, for the tremendous love and light they bring to my life. It is an absolute joy to witness you growing into the powerful young women you are today.

I want to thank my partner, Heddy Hill, for her support, love, and encouragement. Her smile brightens the room and brightens my heart, always.

Last, I want to thank my mom and dad, Karen and Lee Holden Sr., for believing in me, for helping me be the best version of myself, and for raising me with such open minds and open hearts. Who knew that when you combined an aerobics instructor and a judge, you'd get a Qi Gong teacher?

Notes

The Myth That Faster Is Better
1. Lindsey Mulrooney, "Nearly 2 Million US New Cancer Cases Expected in 2022," *American Journal of Managed Care*, July 5, 2002, ajmc.com/view/nearly-2-million-us-new-cancer-cases-expected-in-2022.
2. "Depressive Disorder: Depression," World Health Organization, March 31, 2023, who.int/news-room/fact-sheets/detail/depression.

Choosing Bliss over Busy
1. Shawn Achor, *The Happiness Advantage: How a Positive Brain Fuels Success in Work and Life* (New York: Crown Business, 2010), 15–23.

Stress: Your Modern-Day Inheritance
1. "Stress Management for the Health of It," National Ag Safety Database by Clemson University, 1997, February 1997, nasdonline.org/static_content/documents/1445/d001245.pdf.

Are You Stressed?
1. "Signs and Symptoms of Stress," Mind, accessed December 12, 2023, mind.org.uk/information-support/types-of-mental-health-problems/stress/signs-and-symptoms-of-stress/.
2. "Signs and Symptoms of Stress," Mind.
3. "Stress Facts and Statistics," Recovery Village, August 24, 2023, therecoveryvillage.com/mental-health/stress/stress-statistics/.

4 Catherine Woodyard, "Exploring the Therapeutic Effects of Yoga and Its Ability to Increase Quality of Life," *International Journal of Yoga* 4, no. 2 (July–December 2011): 49–54, ncbi.nlm.nih.gov/pmc/articles/PMC3193654/.

The Bear and the Big Silver Lining of Stress

1 Beth Shaw, "When Trauma Gets Stuck in the Body: How Do We Heal?," *Psychology Today*, October 23, 2019, psychologytoday.com/gb/blog/in-the-body/201910/when-trauma-gets-stuck-in-the-body.

Autopilot and the Drunken Teenage Monkey

1 Suzana Herculano-Houzel, "The Human Brain in Numbers: A Linearly Scaled-up Primate Brain," *Frontiers in Human Neuroscience* 3 (2009), ncbi.nlm.nih.gov/pmc/articles/PMC2776484/.

A Thank-You Note

1 Robert A. Emmons and Robin Stern, "Gratitude as a Psychotherapeutic Intervention," *Journal of Clinical Psychology: In Session* 69, no. 8 (2013): 846–855, static1.squarespace.com/static/54694fa6e4b0eaec4530f99d/t/565f5969e4b05a14ac75ee6c/1449089385801/Gratitude+as+a+Psychotherapeutic+Intervention+2013.pdf.

Why Do You Want to Live Here, Anyway?

1 Eckhart Tolle, *The Power of Now: A Guide to Spiritual Enlightenment* (London: Yellow Kite Books, 2001), 35.

Let Go of Control, and Go with the Flow

1 Richard Huskey, "The Science of 'Flow States,' Explained by a Cognitive Science Researcher," ScienceAlert, January 5, 2022, sciencealert.com/the-science-of-why-flow-states-feel-so-good-according-to-a-cognitive-scientist.

2 Roger Jahnke, Linda Larkey, Carol Rogers, Jennifer Etnier, and Fang Lin, "A Comprehensive Review of Health Benefits of Qigong and Tai Chi," *American Journal of Health Promotion* 24, no. 6 (July–August 2010): e1–e25, ncbi.nlm.nih.gov/pmc/articles/PMC3085832/.

Surfing into Flow

1 Mihaly Csíkszentmihályi, "Flow, the Secret to Happiness," TED Talks, February 2004, ted.com/talks/mihaly_csikszentmihalyi_flow_the_secret_to_happiness.

Channeling Your Inner Bruce Lee

1 "Bruce Lee—Be Water [Longstreet]," YouTube, 2012, youtube.com/watch?v=bsavc5l9QR4.

2 Water Science School, "The Water in You: Water and the Human Body," USGS, May 22, 2019, usgs.gov/special-topics/water-science-school/science/water-you-water-and-human-body#:~:text=In%20adult%20men%2C%20about%2060,their%20bodies%20made%20of%20water.

3 Nipaporn Akkarakittichoke, Mark P. Jensen, Andrea K. Newman, Pooriput Waongenngarm, and Prawit Janwantanakul, "Characteristics of Office Workers Who Benefit Most from Interventions for Preventing Neck and Low Back Pain: A Moderation Analysis," *PAIN Reports* 7, no. 3 (May–June 2022): e1013, journals.lww.com/painrpts/Fulltext/2022/06000/Characteristics_of_office_workers_who_benefit_most.16.aspx.

4 "Sitting Is the New Smoking: 'Truly a Silent Killer,'" Sanford Health, February 9, 2023, news.sanfordhealth.org/heart/sitting-is-the-new-smoking-truly-a-silent-killer/.

Why It's Time for You to Go "Au Naturel"

1 "Au Naturel," The Britannica Dictionary, accessed December 16, 2023, britannica.com/dictionary/au-naturel.

2. "Blue Light Has a Dark Side," Harvard Health Publishing, July 7, 2020, health.harvard.edu/staying-healthy/blue-light-has-a-dark-side.
3. Kimberly Holland, Rachael Ajmera, and Alina Sharon, "Obesity Facts in America," Healthline, March 3, 2023, healthline.com/health/obesity-facts.
4. Gaétan Chevalier, Stephen T. Sinatra, James L. Oschman, Karol Sokal, and Pawel Sokal, "Earthing: Health Implications of Reconnecting the Human Body to the Earth's Surface Electrons," *Journal of Environmental and Public Health* (2012): 291541, ncbi.nlm.nih.gov/pmc/articles/PMC3265077/.
5. A. S. Ogungbe, O. H. Akintoye, and B. A. Idowu, "Effects of Gaseous Ions on the Environment and Human Performance," *Trends in Applied Sciences Research* 6: 130–133, scialert.net/abstract/?doi=tasr.2011.130.133.
6. Alexander J. Smalley and Mathew P. White, *Journal of Environmental Psychology* 86 (March 2023): 101955, "Beyond Blue-Sky Thinking: Diurnal Patterns and Ephemeral Meteorological Phenomena Impact Appraisals of Beauty, Awe, and Value in Urban and Natural Landscapes," sciencedirect.com/science/article/pii/S0272494423000038?via%3Dihub.
7. Stephen Hawking, "'Remember to Look up at the Stars': The Best Stephen Hawking Quotes," *The Guardian*, accessed April 2024, theguardian.com/science/2018/mar/14/best-stephen-hawking-quotes-quotations.
8. "Look up at the Sky—the Benefits of Stargazing," Opticall Eyecare, accessed December 21, 2023, opticalleyecare.co.uk/the-benefits-of-stargazing/.
9. "Vitamin Sea: Health Benefits of the Ocean," Ocean Magic Surfboards, January 9, 2023, oceanmagic.co.uk/blog/vitamin-sea-health-benefits-of-the-ocean/.
10. Nora A. Herweg and Nico Bunzeck, "Differential Effects of White Noise in Cognitive and Perceptual Tasks," *Frontiers in Psychology* 6 (2015): 1639, ncbi.nlm.nih.gov/pmc/articles/PMC4630540/.

11 Ye Wen, Qi Yan, Yangliu Pan, Xinren Gu, and Yuanqiu Liu, "Medical Empirical Research on Forest Bathing (Shinrin-yoku): A Systematic Review," *Environmental Health and Preventive Medicine* 24 (2019), environhealthprevmed.biomedcentral.com/articles/10.1186/s12199-019-0822-8.

Going Deeper: Fuel for the Body
1 "Stress and Eating," American Psychological Association, 2013, apa.org/news/press/releases/stress/2013/eating.
2 "Prevalence of Obesity," World Obesity, accessed December 21, 2023, worldobesity.org/about/about-obesity/prevalence-of-obesity.

Why Do We Stuff Our Bodies at the Buffet?
1 Katheen M. Zelman, "Slow Down, You Eat Too Fast," Nourish, accessed December 21, 2023, webmd.com/diet/obesity/features/slow-down-you-eat-too-fast.

Eat S-L-O-W-L-Y
1 Sophie Ireland, "The Most Fast Food–Obsessed Countries in the World, 2023," *CEOWORLD* magazine, December 21, 2022, ceoworld.biz/2022/12/21/the-most-fast-food-obsessed-countries-in-the-world-2023/.
2 "URI Researcher Provides Further Evidence That Slow Eating Reduces Food Intake," University of Rhode Island, October 27, 2011, uri.edu/news/2011/10/uri-researcher-provides-further-evidence-that-slow-eating-reduces-food-intake/.
3 "Eating Slowly Really Does Inhibit Appetite," University of Rhode Island, November 15, 2006, uri.edu/news/2006/11/uri-study-confirms-popular-dietary-lore-eating-slowly-really-does-inhibit-appetite/.
4 Bing Zhu, Yasuo Haruyama, Takashi Muto, and Takako Yamazaki, "Association Between Eating Speed and Metabolic Syndrome in a Three-Year Population-Based Cohort Study," *Journal of*

Epidemiology 25, no. 4 (2015): 332–336, ncbi.nlm.nih.gov/pmc/articles/PMC4375288/.
5 "The Digestive Process: Digestion Begins in the Mouth," University Hospitals, accessed December 21, 2023, uhhospitals.org/health-information/health-and-wellness-library/article/adult-diseases-and-conditions-v1/the-digestive-process-digestion-begins-in-the-mouth.
6 "Why Is It So Important to Chew Your Food?," Intestinal Labs, accessed December 21, 2023, intestinal.com.au/chewing-food.
7 "Why Is It So Important to Chew Your Food?," Intestinal Labs.

Pleasure Through Food
1 J. R. R. Tolkien, *The Hobbit* (New York: HarperCollins, 2011), 288.
2 "How Do Stress and Anxiety Affect IBS?," Livi, February 26, 2022, livi.co.uk/your-health/how-do-stress-and-anxiety-affect-ibs/.

Combating Fast-Eating Habits with Acupressure
1 John Anderer, "Zombie Eating: 88% of Adults Dine While Staring at a Screen, Survey Finds," StudyFinds, July 24, 2019, studyfinds.org/zombie-eating-88-percent-adults-dine-while-staring-at-screen-survey-finds/.
2 Piyush Mehta, Vishwas Dhapte, Shivajirao Kadam, and Vividha Dhapte, "Contemporary Acupressure Therapy: Adroit Cure for Painless Recovery of Therapeutic Ailments," *Journal of Traditional and Complementary Medicine* 7, no. 2 (April 2017): 251–263, ncbi.nlm.nih.gov/pmc/articles/PMC5388088/.
3 Pei Chen, Jing Li, Xiao Han, Dennis Grech, Ming Xiong, Alex Bekker, and Jiang-Hong Ye, "Acupuncture for Alcohol Use Disorder," *International Journal of Physiology, Pathophysiology and Pharmacology* 10, no. 1 (2018): 60–69, ncbi.nlm.nih.gov/pmc/articles/PMC5871630/.
4 Felicity Lillingston, Paul Fields, and Randall Waechter, "Auricular Acupuncture Associated with Reduced Waist Circumference in Overweight Women—A Randomized Controlled Trial,"

Evidence-Based Complementary and Alternative Medicine (2019), ncbi.nlm.nih.gov/pmc/articles/PMC6935794/.

The Breath as Medicine: Taking Your Vitamin O

1 "Glossary of Neurological Terms: Cerebral Hypoxia," National Institute of Neurological Disorders, accessed December 18, 2023, ninds.nih.gov/health-information/disorders/cerebral-hypoxia.

2 "Breathe," Canadian Lung Association, accessed December 18, 2023, lung.ca/lung-health/lung-info/breathing.

3 Richard P. Brown, Patricia L. Gerbarg, and Fred Muench, "Breathing Practices for Treatment of Psychiatric and Stress-Related Medical Conditions," *Psychiatric Clinics of North America* 36, no. 1 (March 2013): 121–140, sciencedirect.com/science/article/abs/pii/S0193953X13000026.

4 Guy William Fincham, Clara Strauss, Jesus Montero-Marin, and Kate Cavanagh, "Effect of Breathwork on Stress and Mental Health: A Meta-analysis of Randomised-Controlled Trials," *Scientific Reports* 13 (January 2023), nature.com/articles/s41598-022-27247-y.

5 Fincham et al., "Effect of Breathwork on Stress and Mental Health."

6 Xiao Ma, Zi-Qi Yue, Zhu-Qing Gong, Hong Zhang, Nai-Yue Duan, Yu-Tong Shi, Gao-Xia Wei, and You-Fa Li, "The Effect of Diaphragmatic Breathing on Attention," *Frontiers in Psychology* 8 (2017), ncbi.nlm.nih.gov/pmc/articles/PMC5455070/.

7 Grzegorz Bilo, Miriam Revera, Maurizio Bussotti, Daniele Bonacina, Katarzyna Styczkiewicz, Gianluca Caldara, Alessia Giglio, Andrea Faini, Andrea Giuliano, Carolina Lombardi, Kalina Kawecka-Jaszcz, Giuseppe Mancia, Piergiuseppe Agostoni, and Gianfranco Parati, "Effects of Slow Deep Breathing at High Altitude on Oxygen Saturation, Pulmonary and Systemic Hemodynamics," *PLoS One* 7, no. 11 (2012): e49074, ncbi.nlm.nih.gov/pmc/articles/PMC3495772/.

8 Allison Aubrey, "Daily 'Breath Training' Can Work as Well as Medicine to Reduce High Blood Pressure," *Morning Edition*,

NPR, September 20, 2022, npr.org/sections/health-shots/2022/09/20/1123500781/daily-breath-training-can-work-as-well-as-medicine-to-reduce-high-blood-pressure.

9 Mike Thomas and Anne Bruton, "Breathing Exercises for Asthma," *Breathe* 10, No. 4 (2014): breathe.ersjournals.com/content/10/4/312.

10 Volker Busch, Walter Magerl, Uwe Kern, Joachim Haas, Göran Hajak, and Peter Eichhammer, "The Effect of Deep and Slow Breathing on Pain Perception, Autonomic Activity, and Mood Processing—an Experimental Study," *Pain Medicine* 13, no. 2 (February 2012), pubmed.ncbi.nlm.nih.gov/21939499/.

11 Yu Liu, Tong-tong Jiang, Tie-ying Shi, Yong-ning Liu, Xiu-mei Liu, Guo-jun Xu, Fang-lin Li, Yue-liang Wang, and Xiao-yu Wu, "The Effectiveness of Diaphragmatic Breathing Relaxation Training for Improving Sleep Quality Among Nursing Staff During the COVID-19 Outbreak: A Before and After Study," *Sleep Medicine* 78 (February 2021): 8–14, ncbi.nlm.nih.gov/pmc/articles/PMC7724962/.

12 James Nestor, *Breath: The New Science of a Lost Art* (New York: Penguin Random House, 2020).

Breathing and Your Emotional Landscape

1 Ravinder Jerath and Connor Beveridge, "Respiratory Rhythm, Autonomic Modulation, and the Spectrum of Emotions: The Future of Emotion Recognition and Modulation," *Frontiers in Psychology* 11 (August 2020), frontiersin.org/articles/10.3389/fpsyg.2020.01980/full.

Breaking the Ice with Wim Hof

1 Radboud University Nijmegen Medical Centre, "Research on 'Iceman' Wim Hof Suggests It May Be Possible to Influence the Autonomic Nervous System and Immune Response," *Science Daily*, April 22, 2011, sciencedaily.com/releases/2011/04/110422090203.htm.

Why You Need to Shut Your Mouth

1. Christos Georgalas, "The Role of the Nose in Snoring and Obstructive Sleep Apnoea: An Update," *European Archives of Oto-Rhino-Laryngology* 268, no. 9 (September 2011): 1365–1373, pubmed.ncbi.nlm.nih.gov/21340561/.
2. Juliette Tamkin, "Impact of Airway Dysfunction on Dental Health," *Bioinformation* 16, no. 1 (2020): 26–29, ncbi.nlm.nih.gov/pmc/articles/PMC6986941/.
3. George Catlin, *Shut Your Mouth and Save Your Life* (London: N. Trübner & Co., 1869), 30.
4. Tamkin, "Impact of Airway Dysfunction on Dental Health."
5. Tamkin.
6. Ashwin Kamath, Rathnakar P. Urval, and Ashok K. Shenoy, "Effect of Alternate Nostril Breathing Exercise on Experimentally Induced Anxiety in Healthy Volunteers Using the Simulated Public Speaking Model: A Randomized Controlled Pilot Study," *BioMed Research International* (2017), hindawi.com/journals/bmri/2017/2450670/.

Connection: The Self and Others

1. Shimon Saphire-Bernstein and Shelley E. Taylor, "Close Relationships and Happiness," University of California, Los Angeles, Research Gate, January 2013, researchgate.net/publication/283087013_Close_Relationships_and_Happiness.
2. RuPaul, "If You Can't Love Yourself, How in the Hell You Gonna Love Somebody Else?," YouTube, 2018, youtube.com/watch?v=l8AyBlNpePQ&ab_channel=DenesFernando.

Cultivating Slow, Deep Connections with Others

1. "Relationships and Community: Statistics," Mental Health Foundation, accessed December 21, 2023, mentalhealth.org.uk/explore-mental-health/statistics/relationships-community-statistics.

Slow Communication

1 "Active Listening," University of Southern California, March 2020, http://gwep.usc.edu/wp-content/uploads/2020/03/FastFacts-Telephone-Skills-Training-Active-Listening.pdf.
2 Brené Brown, *Daring Greatly: How the Courage to Be Vulnerable Transforms the Way We Live, Love, Parent, and Lead* (New York: Penguin Random House, 2015), 2.

Slow Intimacy

1 Kara Mayer Robinson, "10 Surprising Health Benefits of Sex," WebMD, January 16, 2024, webmd.com/sex-relationships/sex-and-health.
2 "How Sex Makes You Look and Feel Better," SAGA, September 3, 2019, saga.co.uk/magazine/life/how-sex-makes-you-look-and-feel-better.

About the Author

Lee Holden is a globally renowned meditation instructor and wellness pioneer specializing in Qi Gong. As the founder of Pacific Healing Arts, one of Northern California's premier wellness practices, he has earned international acclaim for his dedication to spreading ancient Taoist teachings while maintaining their authenticity.

Lee has been recognized by the International Qi Gong Association for his exceptional contributions. His impact extends across continents, from his keynote speeches in the United States to his stress-management consultancy for Silicon Valley corporations like Apple and 3COM. With television shows reaching fifty million households, including the upcoming syndicated series *Your Fountain of Youth*, Lee continues to influence and inspire countless individuals on their wellness journeys.

Lee is the esteemed author of *7 Minutes of Magic: Recharge Your Body Each Day with Qi Gong*, *Taoist Sexual Secrets*, and *Slow: How to Improve Your Energy, Health, and Relationships Through the Power of Slow*.

Residing in Santa Cruz, California, Lee embraces an active lifestyle as a mountain biker, paddleboarder, and nature enthusiast while sharing his expertise through live classes and studio productions that reach thousands worldwide.

To find out more about Lee and his classes, trainings, and videos, visit holdenqigong.com.